SOMETHING GOOD'S GONNA HAPPEN

PAUL ORBERSON

with

David Mills & Randy Mills

Published by Hi-Hope Publishing Company, LLC

Published in the United States by Hi-Hope Publishing Company, LLC, Georgetown, Kentucky

Book design by Sumo Design, LLC
www.sumodesign.net

Cover photograph © Lee P. Thomas Photography
Additional color photography © Lee P. Thomas Photography
www.leethomasphotography.com

Articles reprinted with permission of the *Danville Advocate Messenger* (pages 84, 93).
Article reprinted with permission of the *Lexington Herald-Leader* (page 94).
Article reprinted with permission of the *Louisville Courier-Journal* (page 84).

ISBN-13: 978-0-9790286-0-1 (paperback)
ISBN-10: 0-9790286-0-4 (paperback)

ISBN-13: 978-0-9790286-1-8 (hardback)
ISBN-10: 0-9790286-1-2 (hardback)

PRINTED IN THE UNITED STATES OF AMERICA

"I have always believed God's favor is just around the corner in my life. If I just keep working harder, if I just don't give up, something good's gonna happen. I realize there is a master plan."

—Paul Orberson

To God Almighty, I will forever thank Him and honor Him daily for the blessings in my life. My inspiration and purpose for everything is Sarah and Jeffrey, and so it is again with this book. Sheryl is my support and my reason for moving forward in this world.

Contents

INTRODUCTION

1: There Is No Right Side of the Tracks 9

2: Life is Short 23

3: You Can't Be Serious 31

4: Start Out Before You Know the Turn Out . . 43

5: Yesterday's History 53

6: The Million Dollar Test 63

7: Some Assembly Required 73

8: Competing for the National Title 95

9: Fundamentals Work 107

10: Calling Your Own Shots 119

11: It's Scripture 131

12: One Hundred Times Better! 143

13: Can Lightning Strike Twice? 153

REFLECTIONS 163

PAUL'S VIEW 171

ACKNOWLEDGMENTS

INTRODUCTION

At the age of thirty-nine, Paul Orberson was a retired multi-millionaire. Yet, when I first met Paul in the late 1980's, he was a high school teacher and coach (painting houses and raising a tobacco crop on the side) struggling to make financial ends meet for himself and his family. Even then, I was impressed with Paul's "giving" spirit, his desire to help and to give to others. To this day, a spirit of generosity characterizes my friend, Paul Orberson.

On November 11, 1990, Paul was introduced to and signed up as a representative with Excel Telecommunications, an up-and-coming network marketing company. That was the beginning of Paul striving for and achieving the American Dream of financial independence.

The realization of his dream was not without struggles and hardships. In fact, after just eighteen months with Excel, Paul wanted to quit and actually tried to sell his network marketing business. However, Paul persevered and within the next three-and-one-half years became the most successful network marketer in the shortest amount of time in the history of the network marketing industry. Indeed, in April of 1996, Paul's monthly earnings topped $1,000,000 for the first time—that's one million dollars a month!

So at age thirty-nine, Paul Orberson, having fulfilled his dream of financial independence, retired. But retired, Paul Orberson could not stay! How come? Because Paul still had a dream. Not just a dream of making more money and adding to his personal fortune, but a dream of "giving back" to people – specifically, a dream of providing "regular people" like himself with an opportunity to better themselves financially and to have more balanced, fulfilled lives.

In Winnie the Pooh, there is a scene where Pooh Bear and Piglet take an evening walk. For quite some time, they walk without speaking, just enjoying each other's company. Finally, the silence is broken by Piglet who asks: "Pooh, when you wake up in the morning, what's the first thing you say to yourself?"

"What's for breakfast?" answers Pooh. "And what do you say, Piglet?"

"I say, I wonder what exciting new thing is going to happen today?"

Small expectations produce meager results. Small dreams yield small accomplishments. Pooh had a "breakfast dream." His dream was too small. His dream was to be content with the way things were. His dream was to focus on the routine and ordinary—breakfast for him was an everyday occurrence. A breakfast dream does not challenge us to fulfill our potential. A breakfast dream is indeed too small.

But an excitement dream? Well, that's another matter. Excitement dreams are visionary enterprises. They do not focus on "how to keep things as they are," but on "how to make things better." Excitement dreams are not content with the routine and the ordinary (the same old, same old); rather they call for well-planned strategies that demand the utilization of resources and the development of potential.

Paul Orberson is an "excitement dreamer." Though financially secure and more-than-comfortably retired at age thirty-nine, Paul soon realized that he could not live the rest of his life on ordinary and routine "what's for breakfast" dreams. He felt led by God to dream a new dream—an excitement dream that would motivate him to use his God-given gifts in network marketing to help other people by providing them with the opportunity to attain financial security.

Paul's new excitement dream resulted in the founding of a new company—Fortune Hi-Tech Marketing. You could say that Paul's new "excitement dream" was and is FHTM. Along with his good friend, Tommy Mills, who also shared Paul's excitement dream, Paul launched Fortune Hi-Tech Marketing on January 5, 2001. To say that FHTM has been successful would be an extreme understatement! Today FHTM is a multi-million dollar company that was recently recognized by *Forbes* Magazine as one of the top twenty-five emerging companies of the decade (the only network marketing company so recognized).

Much more than the financial success of the company, however, Paul consistently emphasizes the primary reason that FHTM was established in the first place: to provide "regular people," (like the once struggling teacher/coach/housepainter/tobacco farmer Paul Orberson) with the opportunity to realize the dream of financial security.

Something Good's Gonna Happen is really the story of a "regular" guy whose life was forever changed for the good because he dared to dream. And in reading Paul's story, he would like nothing better than for you the reader to dare to dream, too—not just a "breakfast" dream, but an "excitement" dream of "what exciting new, good thing is gonna happen today!"

For several years now, I have been privileged to be Paul's pastor. I have also been blessed to have and to know Paul as a close, personal friend. Whenever I think of Paul, there are always several characteristics that immediately surface in my mind.

The first, as previously mentioned, is generosity. Paul is without question one of the most generous human beings that I have ever encountered. He is generous to family, to friends, to FHTM employees, to fellow church members, and to complete strangers. Much of Paul's generosity is done behind the scenes, perhaps never known to anyone else aside from those benefiting from his generous giving. Paul has brightened the day of many a waitress and waiter in restaurants with what undoubtedly was the best gratuity they had ever received. He has made possible for entire Little League baseball teams to attend a major league game. He has anonymously rented out an entire movie theatre so that his church could see an inspirational religious film together. I will never forget the time that he provided a private plane to transport my mother, who had had a heart attack while visiting family out of state, back home. These are just a few of the multitudinous ways that Paul's generosity has positively impacted the lives of other people.

Without fanfare and without drawing attention to himself, Paul is continuously giving and sharing with others. There is a verse of scripture in II Corinthians 9:7 that states: "Each of you must give as you have made up your own mind, not reluctantly or under compulsion, for God loves a cheerful giver." Paul Orberson is a II Corinthians 9:7 Christian: he is a cheerful giver. He exudes a spirit of generosity.

A second trait that characterizes Paul is perseverance. Hebrews 12:1 declares: "…let us run with perseverance the race that is set before us." New Testament scholars tell us that the word translated "perseverance" in this verse is a "strong word, referring to the ability to keep up the stride when the competition is the hardest and the road the roughest." The race track of Paul Orberson's life has not been without obstacles: early financial hardships, the fear of public speaking, the naysayers who questioned his decision to go into network marketing, and his own battle with cancer, just to name a few. But with the help of God and the desire to actualize his dreams, Paul has overcome the obstacles that threatened to steer off track and end his race prematurely. He has "kept up the stride" even during the toughest part of the course. My friend possesses the trait of perseverance.

A third and final characteristic that I must mention in regard to Paul is his faith. Paul has a deep, abiding faith in God. He strives daily (and not just on Sunday at church) to live by the Great Commandment: to love God with all his heart and to love his neighbor as himself (Mark 12:30-31). As his pastor, I can tell you that Paul is faithful in church attendance on Sunday's. But even more importantly, I can tell you that Paul is faithful in "being the church" and in living out his faith Monday through Saturday. You cannot really know or understand Paul Orberson unless you realize that he is a person of faith.

Someone once said that: "Faith is the turning of dreams into deeds." From the perspective of this definition, Paul Orberson epitomizes one who has faith: faith in God, faith in his own abilities to act on the opportunities that God provides, and faith in the ability of "regular people" like himself to achieve their respective dreams, too.

Reading this biography will provide you with a firsthand account of Paul Orberson's amazing story and the story of the incredible success of Fortune Hi-Tech Marketing. It will also convey in layman's language the fundamentals of the network marketing business. More importantly, it will provide you with more than sufficient inspiration to dream your own dreams and more than ample practical motivation to start turning your dreams into reality!

Sprinkled with scripture, true life stories of FHTM Representatives, homespun humor, and practical advice, *Something Good's Gonna Happen* is Paul Orberson's firsthand account of how dreaming excitement dreams has changed his life for the better and enabled him to help others change their lives for the better as well. More simply stated, this book is the story of how my friend Paul Orberson utilizes his God-given talents to make life better for others.

So may you have good reading, and good dreaming. And may you have good fortune in finding the inspiration you need to help you turn your dreams to deeds.

Dr. Robert G. Baker
Pastor
Calvary Baptist Church
Lexington, Kentucky

*　　*　　*

SOMETHING
GOOD'S
GONNA HAPPEN

1

THERE IS NO RIGHT SIDE
OF THE TRACKS

THEY HIT HIM OVER THE HEAD with a baseball bat, knocked him out and dragged him through town to the railroad tracks. They tied his hands and feet to the rails.

Every night at 12:45, just like clockwork, the old L & N # 4 train sped through Gravel Switch, Kentucky, across Highway 68. That night was no different. Except, on that night, the speeding train ran over and killed Marshall Franklin Orberson, my grandfather.

I never met my Grandpa Orberson. Heck, my father never even met him. Marshall Franklin Orberson drifted into Lebanon, Kentucky, in the late 1920's to accept a science teaching position at the local high school. My grandmother, Mamie Matherly, was one of his students.

Fifteen, a sophomore in high school, and scared to death, Mamie became pregnant. Even worse, she had to tell her family that the baby's father was her high school science teacher.

Think about it! In rural Kentucky, in 1930, this was definitely a family matter that required action. Mamie's brothers paid a visit to the schoolhouse to inform Mr. Orberson he would marry their sister. He told her brothers he had absolutely no intention of marrying Mamie.

Well, you can connect the dots and solve this puzzle easily enough. My daddy never met his father and I never knew my Grandpa Orberson.

> *He always told us that God gives us what we need and God feeds the birds every morning, but He doesn't throw the worms down their throats.*

I'm often amused when I hear people talk about being born on "the wrong side of the tracks." I'd say, if we were dogs, most of us would not be any special breed. We would be mutts. You don't have to be a special breed of dog to do something big with your life. You don't have to be born to the right kind of people, go to the right kind of school or grow up in the right neighborhood. Most of us fall into the category of average, everyday, regular people. It really doesn't matter on which side of the tracks we are born. People like us with average intelligence and average ability, with above average desire, can do extraordinary things.

Thank God I wasn't born with a silver spoon in my mouth. My mother, Sheila, and father, Ed, always worked. My mother was nineteen when I was born and soon took a job as a switchboard operator for AT&T. My father was a teacher, painter and a pastor. He taught my brother, Mike, my sister, Karen, and me that work is good. He taught us that work is Scripture. You get up, go to work and good things are gonna happen. He always told us that God gives us what we need and God feeds the birds every morning, but He doesn't throw the worms down their throats. I was raised in a family where God was honored. For that I am grateful.

When I was ten years old, my family moved to Danville, Kentucky, from my birthplace in Lexington. Ironically, my office today is located within minutes of the hospital where I was born, of my first elementary school and of Gardenside Park where I pitched my first baseball game. From the time we moved to Danville, into our house on Alta Avenue, I can't remember a time when I wasn't working or playing ball.

I started a paper route when I was about eleven, delivering the *Danville Advocate Messenger* every day after school. I had a separate morning route with the *Louisville Courier-Journal*. I remember hoeing, cutting, hanging and stripping tobacco season after season on Daddy Jim Yates' farm. When I was twelve I joined one of my father's crews and worked every summer painting houses throughout the county. I worked hard, but I always had time to pursue my childhood passion.

✳   ✳   ✳

Baseball, Basketball, Football. Whatever season it was, I played it. In my senior year, our school baseball team had a record of 26-2. The eventual state championship team from Somerset beat us 4-3 during the regular season. Our other loss came in the state semifinal game to Paducah Tilghman by a score of 1-0. I remember that game well; I pitched. In the bottom of the first there was a man on third with two outs. The next batter hit a ground ball and our third baseman made a throwing error, allowing the man on third to score. The next batter struck out. The score was 1-0 at the end of one inning and it was still one to nothing at the end of the game.

I learned a valuable lesson that day. In baseball, as well as in life, you have to play the entire game, from start to finish. In May of that year at Boyle County High School, I signed a scholarship to pitch baseball for the Western Kentucky University Hilltoppers.

On June 8, 1974, after graduation, I married my childhood sweetheart, Carla Yates, Daddy Jim's daughter. Carla and I moved to Bowling Green, Kentucky, to enter college. At Western I was placed in a remedial reading class, because I had made such a low score on my ACT test. I had to pass the reading class and earn the two credits given for that class in order to continue the next semester. The only reason I was admitted into school in the first place was because, at the time, every student who lived in Kentucky had to be admitted into any state college. I put a lot of effort into the class, knowing that if I didn't pass I would lose my scholarship.

We lived in a mobile home in Skyline Trailer Park. That is, until the "we" became "three." The Bible says, "Sons are a heritage from the Lord." We were blessed with our son, Jeffrey Michael, on December 11, 1974. One week later, on December 18, I turned eighteen.

I forced myself to grow up fast. In my first semester of college I was a newlywed and now a father. I was playing baseball with a full load of classes and holding down a job at a gas station. Still today, when somebody says that I look familiar, I ask them if they may have passed through Bowling Green, Kentucky, in the mid-70's and stopped to get gas at Supertest Gas Station on Morgantown Road. If so, that's why I look familiar; I was the guy checking underneath the hood and filling up their car with gas.

I can remember, clear as a bell, we kept the thermostat at sixty-five degrees during winters in the trailer. We looked forward to taking Jeffrey home to Danville, where the temperature in the house was seventy degrees. We got used to the warmth for a couple of days, then had to return to Bowling Green to start another week of school. It was so cold in January of 1977 that our water heater in the trailer froze and burst. We couldn't afford to get it fixed. For what seemed like months, we heated water on the stove in big cooking pans and added it to cold water in the bathtub each night. The water was lukewarm, at best, but that's how we took baths that winter.

In the summer before my senior year, I was home with my dad going through the same routine. I was still heading out each morning to work on one of his paint crews. I considered how my dad was making a living and I thought it was crazy. He was painting houses, teaching school and still a part-time pastor. I told Dad I wasn't going to be doing three things when I graduated. I said, "I'm gonna get one thing and do it good." Now I realize I shouldn't have been saying those sorts of things to my father, but I remember to this day what he said to me. We were painting a house across from Danville High School at the time and he looked at me and said, "Boy, you'll be lucky to ever make what I'm making if you only do one thing."

Honestly, we were just scraping by at the time, but we didn't think much about it. Life is what it is and there were plenty of other kids back at school doing and going through the same things Carla and I were. Lou Kendall was a catcher on the baseball team and he was my best friend in college. We identified with each other. We were both mutts. I rode my bike to school and finally, in our senior year, Lou got a blue '69 Maverick that we drove everywhere. I'll never forget that car. I said it was blue, but I remember it had more paint peeling off of it than it had on it. Pizza was a big darn deal to us. We would drive out to Ron's Pizza in Bowling Green and that was pretty good, but on special occasions we would go to Pizza Hut. That was the steak of pizza—cheese and hamburger topping on thin crust! Life doesn't get any better than that. To this day, some of the best memories in my life have had nothing to do with money.

As I ended my senior year at Western, I faced disappointment in the two areas I had dreamed of building as a career. First, I was invited to the Cincinnati Reds tryout at Riverfront Stadium and had high hopes of signing a major league baseball contract. Their evaluation? "Don't call us; we'll call you." Since I couldn't do it with my athletic ability, I thought maybe I could do it with my mind. I took the LSAT test for application into law school—twice. I was sent back a nice little note that read, "Sorry, aptitude not present for law." I had worked my tail off, and graduated with a 3.3 grade point average in history and government. Now, I was being told that I wasn't even smart enough for acceptance to law school. My two lifelong dreams had officially been shattered.

I had a professor tell me, "Orberson, you'll never drive a Cadillac teaching school." Well, I never wanted to drive a Cadillac, but after losing both of my career dreams the idea of teaching and coaching sounded like a decent consolation. That seems like a terrible attitude to start a profession with, but that is exactly how I felt at the time. My gross salary when I started teaching in 1978 at Warren Elementary School was $770 a month. It wasn't enough to make ends meet, so I painted houses for five dollars an hour to earn a little extra money.

My teaching and coaching career spanned thirteen years. To this day I greatly respect the importance of the teaching profession. I soon figured out that I loved working with the kids. My father always told me that kids will remember *how you treat them* much longer than *what you teach them*. Teachers are such influential role models in the lives of our children.

From Warren Elementary School we moved to Liberty, Kentucky, where I taught and coached baseball and football at Casey County High School. My path returned me to my hometown when I accepted a teaching position and the basketball coaching job at the Kentucky School for the Deaf in Danville. Toward the end of that basketball season, we were blessed with the birth of our second child. Sarah Elizabeth Orberson was born February 21, 1988.

A job at my high school alma mater became available that spring. Tommy Mills had resigned as the basketball coach in order to become the principal at Boyle County High School. As the new principal, he was in charge of hiring the new coach. Tommy had coached Jeffrey the previous year at Boyle County, but I had known him prior to that time. We were about the same age and had competed against each other in high school and in college on the baseball field. One summer Tommy's team from Frankfort won the Kentucky State Championship, and his team added me to their roster to travel with them to Wisconsin for the National Tournament. Tommy played third base and I pitched. We won a couple of games and lost a couple of games. It was a good experience and my first real introduction to a great friend.

When I took my application to Tommy at the high school, I really didn't have a great resumé for the position. I loved the thought of coaching my son, Jeffrey, at my old high school, but I hadn't proven myself as a basketball coach. I just needed the opportunity at that level. As I thought about the interview, I felt a lot like the little boy who sought an opportunity from the Indian chief. When the boy met with the chief, he simply stated, "Chance."

The chief looked at the boy and said, "No, son. You mean 'how'."

At that the little boy replied, "No, sir. I know how; I just need a chance." Tommy Mills gave me a chance. In three years time, our Boyle County team won the first District Championship in school history.

Yes, I was excited to see how great winning made our kids feel. You know what, though? Financially speaking, I found that I was right smack dab in the middle of doing what my father had done for all those years. I was teaching, coaching two sports, painting houses, and raising a tobacco crop on the side to earn a little extra income for my family. I remember my grandmother, on my father's side, saying my dad was always working a bunch of jobs and now I was just like him. I had become everything that I didn't want to be. I wasn't doing one thing and doing it "good." I was working those three jobs that I told my daddy I never would.

By my late 20's I had quit dreaming. I can remember thinking, "Maybe this is how life is supposed to be." Maybe I was abnormal to think anything great was going to happen to me. I was thinking, "Who are you to have these crazy dreams of being financially independent some day?"

This was my frame of mind when I was invited to see a business presentation on November 11, 1990. Russ Noland came up from Dallas, Texas, to do a meeting for his distant cousin, Brenda Hickey. Jimmy Reed, the football coach at Washington County, Brenda and her husband, Pat, and my former high school baseball coach, Bob Gorley, were there. Russ talked about this company called Excel, and said it was going great.

My initial thought was, "If it's that dadgum good, why is this big company being introduced to the state of Kentucky on a Sunday afternoon in Brenda Hickey's basement?" I was listening and thinking, "I don't have to do this. I'm not that broke; I'm not that destitute; my gosh, I've got a master's degree!" As the talk continued, Russ started writing some pretty big financial numbers on the board. I literally caught myself starting to dream again. I really didn't think I could earn the kind of money Russ was talking about making, but I liked the idea of dreaming. At the beginning of the meeting I was looking around the basement thinking, "This ain't the way greatness is born," but toward the end of the meeting and ever since then I've learned, "This is exactly the way greatness is born."

I signed up with Excel Telecommunications that night. Excel was based in Dallas, Texas, and as representatives of that company we gathered long distance phone customers through a network marketing business model. In other words, I got involved because Russ Noland knew Brenda Hickey; Brenda Hickey knew Bob Gorley; Bob Gorley knew me.

I had some early success in my Excel business and I had some early failures. By the summer of 1991, I decided the only way to really make it in this business was to go full-time and quit my coaching and teaching job. So I did. I devoted full attention to my business and it began to grow, but not nearly fast enough. Carla was still teaching and her paycheck was the only thing that kept us from starving.

"Many of life's failures are men who didn't realize how close they were to success when they gave up."

–Thomas Edison

After eighteen months in Excel, I wanted to quit. I was so beaten down I actually put a price tag on my business and tried to sell it. I was frustrated and at that point I was willing to go back to my comfort zone of coaching and teaching. But since the school year had already started, the prospect of getting back in the classroom would have to wait. I went to Farmers Bank and got a loan to help us get through the next couple of months and I continued to work my business because I had no buyers for it and had no other choice.

Thomas Edison said, "Many of life's failures are men who didn't realize how close they were to success when they gave up." How true that is! Throughout that fall I continued to plug away and plug away, working the fundamentals of my business. In November of 1992, I went from never having made over $1,200 a month, from wanting to quit and sell my business, from nearly starving my family to death, to getting a check from Excel for over $10,000 for that month. That's the power of network marketing.

No one could have calculated what happened next. My checks kept growing as I continued to work the business; each month tens of thousands became hundreds of thousands. Then, in April of 1996, my check went over $1,000,000 for the first time—that's a million dollars for one month's pay! After all that time, I finally found that *my* thing, that didn't look like *my* thing, that I would never have guessed fifteen or twenty years ago to be *my* thing, actually *was my thing*. In three and a half years I had gone from wanting to give up my business to earning more money in the shortest period of time than anyone ever in the history of the network marketing industry.

"Orberson, you're just dang lucky!" I heard it a thousand times. It's amazing how all of a sudden to others you appear to be lucky after years of working your butt off. Of course, they weren't there all those nights that I was driving, and all those nights nobody showed up for business meetings. They weren't there all those nights I missed Jeffrey's high school basketball games. They weren't there all those nights I missed giving Sarah a good night kiss and tucking her into bed. I was sorry every single night I wasn't there. Then several years later, people call me lucky! It's amazing how that works.

I had become financially independent, but it didn't happen without sacrifice. There is no doubt that during this time I lost balance in my life. That loss of balance cost me my marriage. I could have taken a little longer to reach financial independence and I would have had more quality time with my family. Since then I've learned that in order to be truly successful, I must strive for balance in all areas of my life.

I retired at age thirty-nine and moved to southern Florida. The residual income I had built in Excel continued to come in each month. I traveled a lot. I went to the College Baseball World Series with some of my friends from Danville. I went to Yankee Stadium, in New York City, for World Series games. We flew to Atlanta to watch the Braves play. We took a private jet on all our trips, so we could leave for an event a couple of hours before it started, be there, watch it, and be back home that night. Believe it or not, it got old in a hurry.

I moved from Tampa to Long Boat Key to Del Ray Beach. I played a lot of golf and I realized after playing a whole lot of golf that I wasn't getting any better. The toughest thing in my day was trying to figure out where I was going to eat that night. That doesn't sound tough, but it is. I began to realize that a person has to have something meaningful to do each morning when he gets out of bed. I felt like I was living for myself and not giving back.

I wanted to return to my roots. I built a house in Lexington and Sheryl Lamse came up with me to watch the progress of construction. I had been seeing Sheryl through my retirement years in Florida and things were going really well between us. She really liked the house and the Bluegrass State. I decided to sell my house in Florida and move to Lexington. Sheryl and I married in November of 1999, and have had our main residence in Lexington, Kentucky, ever since.

In June of 2000, Sheryl and I sat by the pool at the home of our close friends, Tommy, and his wife, Alane, in Danville. I felt I was beginning to find balance in my personal life, but I was still restless in finding purpose in my daily life. Tommy had also experienced a lot of financial success in Excel. Our circumstances were similar. We both retired at a young age; yet, now we were searching for something meaningful to do with our lives.

Tommy and I have formed the strongest of friendships over the years. In the Bible, when King David was down and out or when he needed a boost, his great friend was Jonathan. Tommy Mills is my Jonathan. We complement each other so well. He has great strengths in areas where I am woefully weak and he tells me that I am strong in his areas of weakness. Tommy is and always has been rock solid.

As we talked and discussed different things we might do with our lives, Tommy said the two of us should start our own company. My first reaction was, huh? I surely don't need that in my life! But Tommy continued to talk and just like at earlier times in my life I started to dream again. Wow! The more we talked and prayed about it, the more I saw this company as perhaps the perfect way to give back to people who had grown up just like I did.

The more we talked and prayed about it, the more I saw this company as perhaps the perfect way to give back to people who had grown up just like I did.

We called Billy Stahl, one of the leaders in Excel. Billy was instrumental in my training with that company and taught me tons about the network marketing industry. We called Ken Wall, a good friend and a top-notch business attorney. We sat down as a group and started making plans.

It was August of 2000 and we still had not chosen a name for the company we were forming. We looked for office space in a building on Fortune Drive in Lexington, Kentucky. We really didn't like the building much, but I loved the name of the street. So much so, in fact, we named our company Fortune Hi-Tech Marketing. We launched our business in a different building, but once we named the company it just seemed like that should have been the name all along.

We all look back on those early days now and smile. The new office didn't have much furniture. Billy Stahl worked on his laptop; Jon Johnson, our Vice President of Product Development, had a cell phone in each ear and one ringing on the table. Ken Wall drew up documents and compared them with what the state required. Barry Levy, my brother-in-law, worked on financial matters, and Tommy took care of hiring our initial staff.

We didn't know what the heck we were going to do at first, but we were so excited about something. That was the most important thing to me. I just had that feeling that something good was gonna happen as the pieces of our Fortune company began to fit together. Earlier I had found my thing was with Excel. In the movie *City Slickers*, one cowboy looks at the other and says the secret of life is "one thing."

The other cowboy looks back and asks, "What is that thing?"

The first cowboy says, "That 'one thing' is for you to find out." We didn't know what this Fortune thing would be, but we knew it wouldn't matter on which side of the tracks a person was born. We were going to provide an opportunity for everyday people to dream again and to find their one thing.

✳   ✳   ✳

2

LIFE IS SHORT

ALTHOUGH I NEVER HAD THE OPPORTUNITY to meet Grandpa Orberson, Lawrence Johnson, my Grandpa Garry, became my hero. He and my grandmother took care of us while Mom and Dad worked. We went over to their house after school and often spent many nights with Nanaw and Grandpa Garry. I used to sit and watch as he took the cheese cutter and carved off big hunks of Velveeta cheese, put it on crackers and ate it every single night. He always washed it down with a glass of good, whole milk.

I've always felt that I got a lot of my traits from Grandpa Garry. He was left-handed. I am left-handed. I have a dark complexion and so did he. He loved sports; he played for his high school basketball team in Kentucky's State Championship game. He was about 5'7", had a medium build and weighed about 160. He was super quick, and I remember him as a really good tennis player, even into his late 50's. I can't even begin to put into words how much I looked up to that man.

Grandpa Garry worked in the men's department at the Hub

Clothing Store on the corner of Third and Main Street in Danville. He dressed sharp and built a large customer clientele. He worked the same job every day, just like the day before, for thirty-one years. Then in 1971 he was told that his commission checks would be frozen and there would be no pay raises for the following year. After punching the clock and working for someone else for more than thirty years, he finally got up the nerve to quit his job and go out on his own.

The Book of James is real clear: "Life is but a vapor that is here today and gone tomorrow."

He began a home remodeling business with my uncle, Johnny Jordan. They started in June and were doing well. They were working hard in and around Danville and had plenty of jobs lined up. But, while remodeling a home on Monday, October 9, 1972, my Grandpa Garry dropped dead from a heart attack—age sixty-one.

For all those years he labored at the Hub and reported to work when someone else told him to. He didn't go home until someone else told him he could. He went to lunch when someone else told him it was time to eat. He had just found the courage, four months before, to leave the Hub. Grandpa Garry was in the process of doing the thing he wanted to do, and just like that, he was gone.

The funeral was on Friday the thirteenth. That night I had a football game against Garrard County. I was fifteen and the closest family member in my life had just passed away. I was almost numb after the funeral. Grandpa Garry had been at every game of every sport that I had ever played. My mind was on everything else but football. I didn't want to play that night.

Everyone said my grandfather would have wanted me to play. So I did. While the results of the game are not important, we did win. I had a date after the game and although I didn't feel like going, I thought it might help get my mind off of things. So I proceeded to go out and I was involved in a terrible car accident. Victor VanArsdale was driving the car and we went over a bridge and rolled thirty feet down a hill onto a railroad track. The train hit the car just after we had all gotten out. I had a large gash across the top of my head that took twenty-four stitches to close, and I spent the night at the hospital in the emergency room.

That week in October of 1972, as a junior in high school, it hit me for the first time that life really is short. I realized that life can be quick for the ones you love and you never know when your life may end in a heartbeat. I learned it by losing the most important family member in my life, and the lesson was reinforced when I nearly lost my own life a few days later. I will never forget the events of that week. Since that time, I have never taken my life or the lives of others around me for granted.

✳　　✳　　✳

What is life? The Book of James is real clear: "Life is but a vapor that is here today and gone tomorrow." We all have that moment, a point when it hits us that life is temporary. For some of us it strikes more than once.

I spent the morning of February 12, 2003, going through my regular workout routine. I lifted weights and did a bunch of push-ups. I ran three miles on the treadmill in under twenty minutes, not bad for a forty-six year old. I couldn't even do that in college; but just three hours later, I doubled over in my living room floor and couldn't stand up. I finally dragged myself to the restroom and my urine was pure blood.

Sheryl took me to the hospital and my vital signs were normal. The first doctor thought I would be fine, but wanted to take an x-ray just to make sure. When the next doctor read the x-ray, he said, "Mr. Orberson, you have something in you that just doesn't look right." It turned out to be a six-pound tumor that had attached itself to my right kidney. Renal cell carcinoma is what the doctor called it. Simply stated, I had kidney cancer.

The doctor told me that the tumor was a very aggressive cancer. It had grown close to the wall of my vena cava. Statistics show that 50% of people can identify with having someone in their lives with cancer. I was now a part of that statistic for the people in my life.

The toughest calls I have ever made were to Jeffrey and Sarah that night. When Jeffrey's phone started to ring I can remember thinking—"This sure ain't the kind of call you want to make to your son."

"Jeffrey, I'm at the hospital."

"What's going on? Are you okay?"

"Well, yeah, I'm all right but they've just told me I have cancer."

"Oh my gosh… no!"

I can't begin to describe the knot in my stomach during that conversation. Would I ever attend another ball game with my son? Would I ever be around to see my grandchildren?

Then I called Sarah, who was fifteen at the time. A thousand thoughts raced through my head as I talked with her. I wanted to see her drive and I wanted to see her graduate from high school. My whole life flashed in front of my eyes. In my mind I could literally see everyone I had ever cared about. I went through the different things I had done in my life and some of the things I still wanted to do. I didn't sleep much that night.

That next morning I was tested from my head to my toes and everywhere in between. I checked into the hospital shortly thereafter.

The tumor, along with my right kidney, was removed on March 2. The tumor was gone, but I developed an infection after the surgery that spread throughout my lymphatic system. I stayed in the hospital thirty days and twenty-nine nights. I weighed a mere 132 pounds when I finally got to go home.

I was tired of the hospital so I was glad to get back into my own bed. Unfortunately, all of a sudden, I started to gain weight. I gained thirty pounds in four days. I knew it wasn't what I was eating, because I couldn't eat any solid food. My lymph nodes were swollen from the infection. My body was not receiving the nutrition it needed. I was retaining fluid. I recall Jeffrey saying, "You're dying right in front of us, Dad. We're taking you back to the hospital right now."

Upon leaving the hospital the second time, the doctors simply believed that it wouldn't be long before the cancer would eat me up. The dying part, if that's what was going to happen, never bothered me. The dying part bothered me because I felt that I would be letting down the ones closest to me. Still, I just couldn't believe that God had brought me to this point to have me die. There had to be more to what was going on. I can remember thinking and really believing that something good was going to come from all of this. Something good had to happen.

I remember people coming by my house to see me lying there in my bed. It was the highlight of my life when Jeffrey, Tommy or anyone would come to see me. Gradually, I got to where I could get up on my own and go to the bathroom. That was a big darn deal. Four months after my surgery, Sheryl still had to help me walk down the steps of our house. We would then work our way back up the steps and I would be so worn out that I would just collapse back into bed. My goal at that point was to be able to walk around my neighborhood at a slow and steady pace.

A couple of months later we were making it around the neighbor-hood pretty well. I had learned so much from the time of my surgery to that point. I read and studied about the disease itself, but the main thing I learned was that I really wanted to live. I never once prayed for God to spare my life. How-ever, I did ask the Lord to move quickly with His plan, whatev-er His destiny may be for me. I was willing to follow whatever steps necessary to get well. I said to myself, "Orberson, you gave yourself this disease. Now with the help of the Lord, you're going to be the one to get rid of it."

"Nothing so focuses the mind like the hangman's noose."
–Benjamin Franklin

I changed my lifestyle. I learned that cancer needed a certain set of criteria to exist within me. I knew I had to put a plan into action to cleanse my body. The things I was supposed to do I started doing and I eliminated many of the don'ts that were in my life. I had faith that God was in control, and He was going to do His part. Now He was waiting on me to do my part.

I stopped chewing tobacco. I stopped smoking. I stopped the ex-cessive exercising. I started eating the foods that would give my body the nutrition it needed. I began to get the rest and the sleep my body craved. Now, I can't imagine my life without having had cancer. By making the necessary changes in my lifestyle, the experience of having cancer, I believe, has no doubt extended my life further than I will ever know. I now belong in the statistical category of cancer survivor!

I sometimes believe that a person is only fit to live after someone, with the credibility to do so, has told them it's imminent they are go-ing to die. "Nothing so focuses the mind like the hangman's noose." Benjamin Franklin made that statement over 200 years ago and it is still true today. During times of trouble, we are really able to focus on the important things in our lives.

This experience with cancer forced me to focus on my personal health, and it became so clear to me that life is more than just one thing. I began to take notice of every aspect of my life. Before cancer, I was successful financially. After the doctor told me there was a cancerous tumor inside my body, I understood pretty well that success in one area of my life does not transfer into any other part of my life. I am subject to the same pitfalls as anyone else.

I have learned to take responsibility for my body and for my overall health. Today, I take no prescription drugs, no treatments, no nothing. I have decreased my over-the-top exercise routine. I don't press as hard as I used to, but I give my body the workout it needs.

I have concluded that a person who has wealth, but no health, is a poor man. Someone with health and wealth, but no relationships, is a poor man. A person with wealth, health and good relationships, but no spiritual direction, is a poor man. As I have focused on each of these aspects of my life, I have learned that balance is the key to success.

Someone might say to me, "Orberson, why didn't you know these things five years ago?" Well, I did, but I failed to prove it with my actions. Today, I don't take anything for granted. I am patiently impatient.

According to Woody Allen, "Ninety-five percent of the people who die today expected to live longer." Having cancer made me, once again, focus on the fact that life is short. We don't have forever to take care of our health. We don't have forever to work on our relationships. We don't have forever to develop our spiritual lives. We don't have forever to build our business. Whatever **IT** is, we don't have forever to do **IT**.

✳   ✳   ✳

You Can't Be Serious

Talk about lasting impressions—I'll never forget my mother's response to the news I shared with her in the summer of 1991. When I announced that I had quit my job to become a full-time network marketer, she looked me dead in the eye and said, "Paul, you can't be serious!"

My mother was scared to death for me. All of my family and close friends were scared for me. And you know what? I was scared, too.

I was twenty-six when I had my first real glimpse of the network marketing industry. In 1981 my father became a representative for A.L. Williams, a network marketing insurance company. I made several trips with my dad to company meetings and seminars. I remember driving to Atlanta to listen to Senior Vice-President Ronnie Barnes speak. He was making $35,000 a month. That was in 1982 when I was teaching school and making about $13,000, a year!

I later met Art Williams, the founder and CEO of the company. I was so nervous. I wanted to say something clever, but I'm sure whatever came out of my mouth sounded stupid because I have no idea what I even said. He called me by my first name and told me that my father was a friend of his. I will never forget how important the president of the company made me feel. That meeting had a big impact on me.

I was not ready to take advantage of the A.L. Williams opportunity at that time in my life, but it certainly shaped my thought process and prepared me for my future in the network marketing industry. I was introduced to people in those early meetings who had been coaches, teachers, doctors and shoe salesmen, among other everyday occupations. Many of these individuals had gone full-time with their network marketing businesses and were earning big monthly paychecks.

It allowed me to dream of financial independence. Nothing else I had tried offered me the big, financial rewards with basically little or no financial risk.

Network marketing provides equal opportunity. It just does. The industry does not reward people for where they went to school. It does not reward a person for who their parents are or are not. It does not reward them for the way they look or for the kinds of clothes they wear.

The principle idea is simple. Representatives bring customers to companies. The customers use the products of that company. The representative is paid a commission generated by each customer's use of the products. Network marketing represents one of the last great ways that a person with average ability, who has an above average desire to work, can accumulate great wealth.

I thought about the financial success of some of the A.L. Williams folks I had met when I decided to go full-time with Excel in the summer of 1991. That's what Excel did for me. It allowed me to dream of financial independence. Nothing else I had tried offered me the big, financial rewards with basically little or no financial risk. Plus, I could participate in this financial dream without having gone to law school!

I was active on the payroll with Excel over the course of about ten years, basically through the decade of the 90's. During that time I personally sponsored a total of thirty-eight representatives into Excel and switched the long distance service of twenty-four customers. My business earned hundreds of thousands of dollars for many months over that period. Yes, there were many months my check topped a million dollars; I certainly felt blessed. But how was so much money generated from the very few people that I had personally brought into the business? What happened?

The basic fundamentals of network marketing were working in my favor. That's what happened. In our business, you personally recruit until you don't have to recruit anymore. I would still be teaching school if I had brought only thirty-five representatives into my Excel business. The beauty of this business model is that while I was working my personal business, my job was to help other people build their business. There are two ways in this country to create wealth—to multiply money or to multiply people. If you don't have any money, then you better take a look at multiplying people.

I think about the industry this way. Picture a football stadium full of $100 bills. Those $100 bills represent the amount we pay as customers for the different types of services and products we use every day. It's not so hard to imagine this scene, because we know that millions of us pay our cell phone bill every single month. We pay our Internet access bill every month. We pay for satellite TV service and for our long distance telephone usage every month. The list goes on and on. All of this money is collected in that football stadium day after day, month after month, year after year.

So I'm standing there outside the fence, looking into the stadium at all that money. Let's say I'm a teacher or a nurse, a factory worker or whatever I am. I stand there and watch as these big trucks come in one after the other and pick up loads of that money each day and haul it out of the stadium. These are nice trucks, too. They are company trucks like Verizon, AT&T and Dish Network, and they are taking the money we have paid for their services back to headquarters to distribute as they choose. The stadium is completely emptied by the end of each day, then every night a whole new pile of $100 bills is placed back into the stadium.

I watch those trucks carry out huge loads of money every day. I begin to think that maybe it would be nice if I could carry out just a bucket or two of those bills each day. I see various individuals go into the stadium and fill up small trucks with money, while some just fill up a wheelbarrow or a bucket. Again, I think, if I could just have a small part of that, it would be enough for me. I don't need that whole stadium. But, how the heck can a little guy like me get a piece of that lucrative pie?

Thank goodness a friend of mine told me that it only costs about $299 to purchase my own network marketing business, allowing me to gain access to the stadium. I don't need a Harvard education, don't have to be a straight-A student, don't even need to be born on the "right" side of the tracks to get in. If I want to market a few of the services that we all use every day, I could start to carry some of that money out of the stadium.

Hmm! This process is going on day after day with or without me. There are people working their own network marketing business, bringing customers to those big companies and carrying out some of those $100 bills each day. I can choose to participate or I can continue to stand and watch from outside the fence.

Sure enough, though, your brother-in-law says he's not gonna do that. He knows somebody that got burned by network marketing.

Great, that's fine. Then he needs to go start his own cell phone company, if he wants to compete in the arena of financial independence. He needs to look into buying a burger franchise and work a heck of a lot of hours for his paycheck. Tell him he will need a whole lot more than $299 for the opportunity to build lasting wealth for his family and himself.

Free enterprise goes to a different kind of person. I read in *USA Today* that people who earn between $150,000 and $250,000 a year are three times more likely to have gone to professional school. A person who makes between $75,000 and $150,000 a year is three times more likely to have completed a bachelor's degree. At an income level of $75,000 and below, a person will probably have the equivalent of a high school diploma or an associate degree.

Those are nice, neat categories that provide an idea of the average salary of individuals based on the amount of education they have. However, look at what happens in the real world. For someone who earns over $400,000 a year, all of the educational figures break down. An individual earning over $400,000 a year is no more or no less likely to have even attended college. This tells me that to make it big financially, personal desire and commitment to success are the most important factors.

When Tommy and I made the decision to start Fortune in the summer of 2000, we wanted to build a different kind of company for a different kind of person. We both believe you win in every area of life with fundamentals. We wanted to build our company with strong fundamentals. We wanted to keep the company private, keep the company debt free, keep shareholders out of it, keep banks out of it and offer products tied to no particular industry or no one company.

When I went to my mother and let her know of the plans to start my own company, she told me, "Son, you got the world by the tail.

You are retired; you've got no worries. Now you want to get up, go to work, fly around the country doing meetings again. Paul, you can't be serious!" I couldn't wait to get started.

It took about six months from the time Tommy and I talked in the summer of 2000 to plan and prepare for our company to open. It was such an exciting time as we worked on staffing and prepared our office for business. We launched Fortune Hi-Tech Marketing on January 5, 2001. Over 1,500 people packed in for the opening night meeting to listen to the opportunity we had designed for them.

Our company opened with four product services in January of 2001. We had voice mail, websites for our representatives, paging and long distance services. We worked with Ron Way from a company called Fionda. It certainly helped us to get out of the gate in a big way. We did a solid job for the first six months and other companies began to contact us to market their products.

Our product line grew to six offerings with the addition of Cingular Wireless and Dish Network in September of 2001. I was traveling a lot, conducting meetings in Columbus, Little Rock, Atlanta and many other cities. We were handling calls at the home office, sending out materials, and Glenn Gatewood, our Director of Commissions, was distributing checks to our representatives on time. The Fortune business model seemed to be strong. The fundamentals of our business seemed to be strong, but our bottom line started out weak.

I remember meetings Tommy and I had in the early months of Fortune focusing on the huge initial costs to get the business started. Never, as a company, have we had a losing financial year, but there were months early on that the company lost chunks of money. I mean big chunks. Tommy and I took a look inward. We questioned ourselves, "Do we really know what we are doing?"

Honestly, there were times when it would have been a whole lot easier just to shut the business down. Tommy and I don't think that way, though. As we talked about it we always ended each and every meeting the same way: "It's gonna be okay." Sometimes Tommy assured me it was going to be okay and other times I assured Tommy it was going to be okay. We always ended a negative bottom line meeting with that thought— "It's gonna be okay." We knew the fundamentals of our business were strong. We

Teddy Roosevelt believed, "If you have a problem, do what you can, where you are, with what you have."

always believed that over a period of time something good was gonna happen.

Fortune did struggle as a company initially. I struggled in the early stages of my Excel business. Teddy Roosevelt believed, "If you have a problem, do what you can, where you are, with what you have." This business is a challenge for the company as well as for the representative, but we reap what we sow. It is only when we survive the tough times that we are able to realize the fruits of our labor.

When I hear of people struggling to build their own business, I think of the process our company went through to open Canada for our representatives. There were so many times during 2004 and 2005 that we thought we were ready to do business there, but each time we had to push the launch date back.

Finally, after enduring months and months of red tape, Fortune opened for business in the Canadian market. Gilbert Anderson, from Alberta, was there and he believed in the Fortune opportunity. He had his organization ready when Canada finally opened in November of 2005. He held his group together as we battled the long, legal process to do business there.

Gilbert is an extremely hard worker and a great leader, but it was difficult from the beginning for his group, as well as for him. Before we were able to open Canada for business, other companies offered Gilbert and members of his organization big money to join them. When we did open there, our representatives had only two products to market and the initial fee was more for a representative to participate in Canada than it was in the United States. Still, Gilbert would not be denied.

I'm not sure I would have made it, if I had to struggle through all the barriers Gilbert and his group had to overcome. But Gilbert Anderson is tougher than a striped snake. It takes a special kind of person to hold on to that focus. I'm sure he was pleased when he received a Fortune check that reached above five figures for the first time. About eight months later, six of the leaders in his organization earned new Lexus model cars, courtesy of Fortune, for the level of business each individual had produced. I know Gilbert was even more excited for the success of others within his organization than he was for his own success.

Gilbert has said the main reason he felt Fortune was the best opportunity out there for him and his organization was that he believed, through his extensive research into the industry, that Fortune was a company that would be around to finish the deal. Fortune pays out millions of dollars a month to its representative base, which in turn gathers loyal customers within the different product areas we offer. I believe with all my heart and soul that Fortune is and will be the best opportunity for the little guy to create wealth in this country now, and for many years to come.

Gilbert's business has spread deep into the western United States, where he currently works with a number of outstanding leaders. Gilbert told me that he believes there will be Fortune Representatives who will make more money in their business than I did in Excel. I have no doubt that he could be one of them, and no one will be happier than me when that happens.

✳   ✳   ✳

Each representative has an equal opportunity for financial success in this business. However, if I had not done well in network marketing it wouldn't have meant the opportunity was not good. No, no, no. The opportunity was, and still is as good as ever, even if the results for me may not have been good. A person's result does not change the magnitude of the opportunity. Network marketing guarantees equal opportunities; it does not guarantee equal results.

In the corporate office we go through mixed emotions, highs and lows, while following the businesses of all of our Fortune Representatives. We live and die a hundred times each month. We are so pleased to see representatives like Sheri Winter and Darla Christianson receive monthly Fortune checks in excess of $30,000. Others are bringing home monthly checks in the hundreds of thousands of dollars and that's great. We are just as excited and proud when someone like Michael Chorost, who recently wasn't even on the radar screen, jumps up and receives a check for over $8,000. Yet, we are very disheartened when we see one of our representative's checks decrease from the previous month.

Each of us realizes the effort it takes to make this opportunity work for our representatives. And while we at Fortune are a dysfunctional family at times, we are a family. We will never be perfect, but we will never claim to be. Over the long haul our goal is to get it right and to provide a company with the financial stability to be there for our representatives.

In the Book of Proverbs, the Bible says, "Lean not on your own understanding." There has to be an element of faith involved. I wondered if we could make this thing work during Fortune's early struggles. I didn't want this company to fail. I knew its success or failure is what I would be remembered for. These were the same thoughts that dominated my mind in my early days with Excel. I realize these are the same hurdles our Fortune Representatives struggle with in the early stages of their own business.

> *The American dream is alive and well. I am a product of that dream. I lived it firsthand.*

I don't believe it's true when I hear people say, "You can't do what you used to do in this country," or, "It's not possible to really climb the ladder of success anymore." The American dream is alive and well. I am a product of that dream. I lived it firsthand. The American dream is better than ever for people who work hard and position themselves properly in front of something big.

From the beginning, the Fortune business model aimed to position our company as a leader in the network marketing industry. Fortune is rapidly growing. We just closed this past year with a profitability margin of five times the previous year. Our representatives have one of the best pay plans in the industry. In fact, I would be willing to compare our top wage earners against any other network marketing company.

Fortune Hi-Tech Marketing offers a big opportunity. Network marketing itself offers us an equal playing field. We can compete for financial independence, regardless of our education or our "place" in society. We can create wealth for our family, without having to mortgage the house or dip into the children's college fund. Each and every one of us can walk into the stadium and carry out $100 bills, if we are only willing to do the necessary work.

I have experienced the network marketing industry as both a representative and as a company owner. This business is not easy; nothing worth fighting for is. Perhaps the biggest struggle we face is to overcome the preconceived notions of network marketing, and we can all name that tune, "You're doing what? You can't be serious!"

✳   ✳   ✳

START OUT BEFORE YOU KNOW THE TURN OUT

THE LAST THING CHRIS DOYLE WANTED was to attend a network marketing business presentation.

Prior to 1997, Chris was a successful business owner for the largest apparel contractor of stonewashed blue jeans in the United States. His company generated millions of dollars a year in business and Chris earned a seven-figure income during that time. He and his family didn't worry about the cost when they went on vacation. They didn't worry about the balance of their bank account; they knew money was there for whatever they wanted. Chris and his family lived a different lifestyle than most people.

Then in 1996 life changed for Chris. The North American Free Trade Agreement was signed. His factory couldn't compete in the world market where foreign labor was cheap, and his company filed for bankruptcy within eighteen months. Just like that, he went from being on top of the world to the lowest point in his life.

Chris was in his mid-40's and had to start over. He became depressed and felt he was letting his family down. His wife, Judy, went back to work. The family struggled and Chris suffered through a long period of self-doubt.

In the early months of 2002, his nephew asked him repeatedly to take a look at the Fortune Hi-Tech Marketing overview. Three times Chris had said he would come to a meeting, but three times he didn't show. Out of guilt he finally attended a Fortune meeting. Before the meeting he stood outside the door and felt like he was wasting his time. He thought he would be looking at some kind of stupid business or pyramid deal.

> *"The secret to getting ahead is to get started."*
>
> *–Mark Twain*

Chris had never considered network marketing as a legitimate business, but after seeing the plan, the Fortune program changed his mind. He didn't fully understand the compensation plan or the bonus plan at first, but he certainly understood the concept of the business. He couldn't come up with a reason why it wouldn't work. He wasn't sure if he could succeed in network marketing; all he knew was that he needed some extra income.

The good news for Chris was that it cost just $299 to own his Fortune business. He knew, from his eighteen years of experience in the manufacturing business, that there was no way he could start again in a conventional business for that small amount of money. Plus, after his bankruptcy, there was no bank in the country that would have given him a business loan.

He started to meet with Fortune Representatives who were doing well in the business. He figured he might not be as good as they were, but with time and effort he could learn. He treated his Fortune business like a full-time business. He remembered it was about four and a half years before his jeans company began to make big profits, so he didn't expect success overnight.

Soon, Chris began to see his hard work rewarded in the form of a Fortune paycheck. He was able to financially contribute to the family again, by paying some of the monthly bills. Even though his wife had not initially been in favor of him working the Fortune business, she became his strongest supporter after seeing the positive, mental impact the work and its rewards were giving her husband. I recognize one of the most important steps for building a successful business in Chris Doyle's story.

"Paul, what's the secret to success in network marketing?" That's the question I'm asked everywhere I go. I don't know any secrets. Success isn't assured by just one thing. When I sat in Brenda Hickey's basement and listened to the Excel presentation, I never imagined where network marketing would take my life. What I do know is that I had to start out with my business before I could know how it was going to turn out. That's the key!

Mark Twain once said, "The secret to getting ahead is to get started." That was the most important step for me, just to get started in my own business. I already knew how each day started in teaching and coaching. I also knew at the conclusion of the day, financially, how it was going to end. I was not satisfied; I desired something more.

I started my Excel business not knowing how it would turn out. Tommy and I started Fortune Hi-Tech Marketing also not knowing how it was going to turn out. Chris Doyle started his Fortune business not knowing how it was going to turn out either.

Today, Chris is a leader in our Fortune company as a National Sales Manager and Presidential Ambassador. He earns hundreds of thousands of dollars a year. Now, he and his family enjoy financial success after overcoming many setbacks and struggles early in his career. The most important decision Chris made in March of 2002 was to get his business started. However, starting out before you know the turn out is not easy.

* * *

I never believed in writing down goals, but I was asked to list them at an Excel training school in February of 1991. I was at the Marriott Griffin Gate in Lexington, Kentucky, and our trainer, Billy Stahl, who has forgotten more about network marketing than I will ever know, thought that would help us with our focus. I wrote down three goals. The first goal was that I wanted to pay off the Nissan truck I was driving. The second goal was to save $25,000 in an emergency fund for my family. My third goal was to have a clear title to my house, all bought and paid for. At the time those looked like huge goals to me. Since then I've had people say, "My gosh! That's all you wanted?"

Some "successful people" say they always knew exactly what they wanted. They wrote their goals down and taped them on the mirror or kept their goals written on a calendar to review each day. Well, to me that's saying that if I don't have those thoughts or I don't know what I want to do or if I don't write down my goals, then I can't be successful. My true goals, Sarah and Jeffrey, I didn't need to write down; they were etched into my heart.

I don't think you need to know what you want out of life, because the things you want will change. I think you need to know exactly what you don't want out of life.

I thought I wanted to live in the plush neighborhood of Avila in Tampa, Florida. I wasn't happy there. I thought Clearwater looked like the dream place to live, but in less than two years I was looking for something else. I thought it was a great dream for a Kentucky boy to live on the beach, so I bought a house on the island of Del

Ray. I was a hundred feet from the ocean when I stepped off my back porch. I guess we get used to what we get used to and in four or five months I stopped making the effort to even go to the beach anymore.

I moved from the beach house after a year. All of the material things I've wanted in my life have changed.

When my grandfather, whom I still love and respect as much as anybody who has ever walked this earth, died, he didn't have anything monetarily to leave for my grandmother. My parents had to assist her financially so she could continue to live in her own house. That made a big impression on me and was one of the driving forces that always made me strive for something more to secure the financial future of my family.

I don't think you need to know what you want out of life, because the things you want will change. I think you need to know exactly what you don't want out of life.

I have found that I have been the most successful in my life when I have focused on the things I didn't want. In 1990 I didn't want to paint houses or raise a tobacco crop. I was tired of it. I didn't want a big truck payment each month. I didn't want to live paycheck to paycheck. I didn't want to go into debt to send my kids to college. I didn't want my family to be broke when I turned sixty.

Those things I didn't want in my life motivated me to start my Excel business. I didn't start out in Excel to be a millionaire. At that point in my life I just simply refused, financially, to live an ordinary life. We all make up our minds to accept things as they are, or to change the things we don't want and start out on a new course.

I wasn't immediately comfortable approaching people about my new business, but once I committed to going full-time I knew I had to do just that. I quickly learned that I was simply sharing with others what I was doing; I wasn't forcing anything on anybody. I also learned that my sincere belief in what I was doing, truly striving to help others, allowed me to develop meaningful relationships well beyond the business realm.

In the early stages of my Excel business, I bumped into Dr. Ken Wall at the Danville Post Office. Dr. Wall was my elementary school principal. Our paths crossed occasionally during my years of teaching and coaching but I hadn't seen him for some time. We chatted for a few minutes. He was aware that I had given up coaching, and asked what I was doing. It was still difficult for me to share my business venture, mainly because of the perception I knew some people had of network marketing. I had been visible in the community as a teacher and coach, and now I had to tell my friends that I was a representative of a network marketing company.

I always admired and respected Dr. Wall. I got around to telling him that I was working a business called Excel. I asked him if he knew anyone in the Louisville area, because I wanted to get my business started in Kentucky's largest city. He said his son was an attorney there, and I was pleasantly surprised when he said the business sounded interesting enough to him that he would like to travel to Louisville with me to meet with his son.

Far beyond Excel business matters, an enduring friendship with Dr. Wall and his entire family blossomed from that initial talk at the post office. We took numerous trips together and enjoyed some wonderful talks. Most of our conversations had nothing to do with business. His son, Ken, became a great friend as well, and would later play an integral role in the opening of our Fortune Hi-Tech Marketing business.

Building relationships! Imagine the loss in my life if I had not shared "what I was doing" with Dr. Wall. In its simplest form, network marketing is actually a friendly conversation waiting to happen. I've found that my most cherished possessions over the years with network marketing experiences have been the relationships that I have formed and developed. These are friendships that I would never have had if I had not started down the path. I would have never met so many of the people who are in my life today, if it had not been for Excel.

*   *   *

In our Fortune business today, Steve and Miranda Bruce come to my mind when I think of starting out and charting a new course. Steve worked for Wal-Mart in the management level of a local store in southwestern Missouri for thirteen years. Miranda worked as a nurse for fifteen years. They earned about a hundred thousand dollars a year, but with six children there never seemed to be quite enough time or money to do all the things they wanted.

They became Fortune Representatives, and at the end of the third month in the business Steve resigned from Wal-Mart. In month five of their business, Miranda followed by giving up the nursing field and they both went full-time working their Fortune business as a team. Their financial success has been remarkable and they replaced their previous salaries in less than a year with Fortune.

Miranda grew up on a dairy farm and Steve never attended college. They had never been in any other network marketing program. They basically had no knowledge of the industry. They just had a mountain of desire and tons of enthusiasm.

Steve and Miranda Bruce took a leap of faith and started their Fortune business without any idea how it might turn out. Like so many in the Fortune family, Steve and Miranda are just good, solid, wonderful people and I know they work their Fortune business for more than the financial rewards. I know from being around them that they are taking pleasure in helping others get started in their businesses.

I truly believe that everyone wants to own more of his or her own time, and I believe owning your own business is the only way to eventually gain more control of your day-to-day schedule. I stirred up a feeling of hope inside of me that tomorrow was going to be better than today when I started out in Excel.

Hope is the feeling you get that the feeling you've got, ain't permanent.

I believe hope is a good thing. I believe dreaming is a good thing too! But all the hoping and dreaming we do won't amount to a hill of beans if we don't take action.

The Bible tells us that God offered the land of Canaan to the Israelites, but they had to rise up and fight for their new home. Scouts warned the Israelites that men of great stature occupied Canaan and relayed the message that it would surely be difficult to take. The Israelites were scared and made no attempt to even strike a single blow for their Promised Land. God let his people wander in the desert for forty years because they didn't have the faith to start out on what they saw to be too difficult of a battle.

Is this business difficult? **You betcha!**

Is the opportunity there to change your financial life in a big way? **I guarantee it!**

When Tommy and I started Fortune, we both decided that we weren't doing ourselves or anybody else any good in retirement. We didn't want to just sit back and let the world go by. When we started out we risked failure just like anyone else attempting something new.

I think sometimes we see other people who we think are successful and we say this or that about them, simply because we don't like where we are in our lives. Those folks are the same as you and me. They have the same hopes and the same fears. I've found that there is not that much difference in us doing something in a big way or in a small way. The bigger deal we make of it, the bigger deal it becomes.

We all want to know the turn out and therefore we often fail to start out. And it's not just in our business world or in our financial matters. Heavens no! We must have the courage to start whatever it is in our lives we need to start.

We need to start spending more time with our family. We need to start spending more time with our church family. We need to start working our way out of debt. We need to start eating a healthier diet.

After I was diagnosed with cancer I started to take responsibility for my overall health. I decided there were things in my life that I just refused to accept.

Now, I refuse to accept the power of a cigarette pulling me over to the side of the road to take a smoke. I have not had a cigarette in my mouth since the doctor diagnosed me with cancer. I refuse to accept the power of Nicorette pulling me over to buy more gum. I don't want or desire nicotine in my body ever again. I refuse to have bad relationships—life is too short! If I can't have a good personal relationship or a positive business relationship, then I just won't have the relationship at all.

I say you just start out, then go out every day and do the very best you can. I've always heard that the best time to plant an oak tree was forty years ago. *The next best time is today.*

✳   ✳   ✳

YESTERDAY'S HISTORY

BELIEVE IT OR NOT, I had worked my Excel business for almost five months and had not conducted a single business presentation. I had sponsored a few individuals into the business, yet I relied on Bob Gorley to speak at the opportunity meetings. Then one day Bob called and said there was no way he could attend the meeting that night. Uh, oh! I knew what that meant. I would have to make the business presentation myself.

Before the meeting I was so nervous. Actually, I was scared to death! I didn't have enough confidence in myself to give the business presentation. Honestly, I just couldn't talk in front of people.

I still remember one specific church service when I was only nine. It was customary for our pastor to call on someone from the congregation to lead the benediction. One Sunday night there were about 300 people in the First Baptist Church of Danville. I was standing beside my Grandpa Garry, holding his hand, when our pastor asked, "Lawrence, would you close the service with a prayer?" Grandpa Garry stood there and stood there and stood there. Then he started shaking like a baby and never spoke a word.

I will never forget that moment. I was scared for him. After what seemed like an eternity, the pastor finally had to give the prayer. I knew that was one more trait I had inherited from my grandfather. That fear of speaking in public carried right on into my adulthood.

All of us can do something great if we just get out of our own way.... It's not that we can't do great things; it's just that we won't attempt to do great things.

During my years of teaching and coaching in Casey County, I attended the First Baptist Church of Liberty. Our pastor also called on congregation members to close each service on Sunday night. I really hate to admit it, but there were Sunday nights I missed the entire service for fear that he may call on me to pray. I would get my courage up and go back to church by telling myself that if I wasn't a regular, the pastor wouldn't feel like he could call on me to pray.

Art Williams said something like, "Before you can be good at anything you have to be bad first. Before you can be bad you have to start. And before you start, you have to want something more than you have today." There is a series of events that must take place. Most of us just don't start out being good at something. We have to speak to fifteen people in a room before we can be good when there are fifty in a room.

It just so happened there were about fifteen people there the night I gave my first Excel presentation. My heart was pounding. I don't know how long I stood up in front of everyone, but it seemed like forever. Somehow I made it through. Eleanor Roosevelt said, "Do the thing you fear and the death of fear is certain." I became more and more comfortable speaking in front of people after that night.

I pressed on. If anything big-time was going to happen in my life, I was going to be the one to do it. I was never going to inherit a fortune and nobody was going to hand me anything. I felt responsible for my life and where I needed to be. I once read that when we get up every morning, we should take a good look in the mirror because we are looking right at the person who we must outwit, outfox, and outmaneuver, if we ever plan to succeed in our lives.

These words ring true in my life. We are our own worst enemy. All of us can do something great if we just get out of our own way. We underestimate our greatest opponent in life: ourselves.

Educated by Aristotle, perhaps the most renowned philosopher and scientist of the ancient world, Alexander the Great conquered the known world by the tender age of twenty-eight. Alexander is often considered the greatest war leader the world has ever known. He waged war for eleven years of his life and never lost a single battle. Every army known to mankind chased him, with all the high-tech weapons of that day, but none defeated him.

Alexander, however, died before his thirty-third birthday. Throughout his adult life he carried with him a severe drinking problem as well as an out-of-control womanizing problem. Historians differ in their accounts of how he died. Some believe syphilis was the cause of his death, while others insist he fell from his horse while he was drunk, smashed his head against a rock and died.

The Reverend John Hagee says, "That which you refuse to conquer, will conquer you." What no other man could do, Alexander the Great did to himself.

People ask me about teaching school for thirteen years and I always correct them. Really, I taught school one year, thirteen times. Each year I knew I needed to do something else. One year rolled into the next; I was off school for holidays, for part of the summer, and we just get used to what we get used to. By not making a decision to do something else, I made a decision to keep on doing what I was doing.

I had to convince others that I was serious about changing my financial life when I finally did go full-time with Excel. I turned in my resignation to the superintendent, Mrs. Carlton, and she asked me to take my time and think about it. I said, "No ma'am, I don't want to think about it. I feel like this is what I need to do."

Whoa! Now that was a mountain to climb! I had grown up in Danville, gone to grade school and middle school in Danville. I came back as a coach and teacher to Boyle County High School from which I graduated. And there I was, after thirteen years of coaching and teaching, trying to convince my hometown folks that I knew what I was doing in the financial world.

I think others see us as we see ourselves. Most of us, from time to time, feel incompetent. We question whether we are doing the right thing or if someone else could do a better job.

My biggest problem was convincing myself that I knew what I was doing. Most of us shy away from doing things that make us step out of our comfort zone. We simply make our problems bigger when we diminish our own abilities. It's not that we can't do great things; it's just that we won't attempt to do great things.

The Israelites were guilty of diminishing their own abilities as they peered into God's Promised Land of Canaan. Caleb quieted his people and told them to go up at once and take possession of the land while they were able to overcome the enemy. Caleb's troops responded that they were not able to go up against those mighty forces because they were too weak. The scouts spied out the land and reported the inhabitants of the land were great in stature. Therefore, the Israelites saw them and viewed themselves like grasshoppers. In turn, that is how they were seen. In other words, they made their enemies out to be giants.

We sometimes make our enemies out to be giants. Our enemy could be life issues such as maintaining good health, balancing finances, developing good relationships or settling family issues. We only conquer the giants in our lives by facing our fears head on.

I had gone far beyond any financial expectations I ever had for myself when I retired from Excel. I realize now, that with each obstacle I overcame, I was building a stronger foundation for my business. I certainly didn't do everything the right way. No, far from it! I made mistakes. There were times I wanted to quit. But I didn't. I faced my "enemies" and I stayed in the game. One of my favorite quotes is from Teddy Roosevelt: "Far better it is to dare mighty things, to win glorious triumphs, even though checkered by failure, than to rank with those poor spirits who neither enjoy nor suffer much because they live in the gray twilight that knows neither victory nor defeat."

There were certainly some anxious moments when Fortune started. I was once again forced to take off my mask, and to answer some really tough questions. Who am I? What am I trying to do? What if Fortune doesn't work? My gosh, I could fail.

In order to move forward, I had to leave my victories as well as my defeats in the past. There is nothing that will destroy us more quickly than forever boasting about a victory we had in 1996, just as there is nothing that will destroy us faster than obsessing over the business defeat in 1994 that we've never gotten over.

Forget what happened yesterday, forget the victories of the past and forget the failures of the past. Each day, each month and each year represent the chance for a new "start out." Get over it, because nothing will keep you more emotionally, physically and financially broke than constantly thinking about the past. Let's strive to follow one of the guiding principles of Dr. Martin Luther King, Jr., "I'm not the man I ought to be and maybe I'm not the man I could be, but thank God I'm not the man I used to be." We must act in the present.

Starting our own business is a new beginning for most of us. I so often see people in networking who mistakenly think that their success as a lawyer or as a coach or as a dentist will automatically translate into success in this industry. That's just not true. Neither is it true that current failure in our financial lives translates into failure in this industry or any other industry.

✳　　✳　　✳

Mike Misenheimer was an Excel representative for ten years. He was in San Francisco when he heard that Excel Telecommunications had officially closed. He received a call from Ruel Morton, one of Excel's top money earners, who was meeting in our office to evaluate joining our company. Mike flew home to Arkansas then drove all night to get to Lexington to see what Ruel was so excited about. Mike and his wife Brenda understand the fundamentals of the business. They are a dynamic team who embrace the overwhelming opportunity presented by this industry.

While Mike and Brenda worked Excel full-time, they were unable to build the level of residual income that would allow them any significant time away from their business. His only job prior to joining Excel was shoeing horses. Mike has seen the tough times and understands the difficult challenges successful people must endure. In his early years of Excel, a fire burned down the garage at his house. He was way behind on paying his bills and was forced to use the $8,900 insurance check to pay bills rather than to rebuild his garage. On another occasion Mike and Brenda wrecked their car while returning home from an Excel convention. Just as before, they used most of the insurance money to catch up on late payments. But throughout these hardships, Mike and Brenda continued to work their business.

Mike tells me he was an average student through his high school and college years, but he is a superior student in the classroom of network marketing. The Misenheimers chose to join Fortune, and in their first six months they built a larger income than they had during all their years in the Excel business. They worked just as hard in their Excel business as they did in the Fortune business, but Fortune's compensation plan allowed them to grow revenue so much faster.

One person I try to emulate is the old-time baseball great, Satchel Paige. He'd say, "It's okay to look back, but just don't stare."

Mike didn't dwell on past history. He didn't look back; his aim was straight ahead. He views the Fortune business as his chance to complete a task, to be done once and for all with his financial worries. He plans to buy T-shirts for his family that simply say "Done" on the front. As his family strolls down the beach, he envisions people asking what "Done" means. He will program his family to respond that they can't talk about it anymore because, "We are done!!"

We carry around a bunch of garbage from our past. Both good garbage and bad garbage keeps us from moving forward in our lives. I've had people say to me, "But isn't it great to remember your victories?" Hey, remember them for the moment, gain confidence, build on your success, then press forward.

Leave our regrets of the past behind. Those regrets lead us into the paralysis of cynicism. One person I try to emulate is the old-time baseball great, Satchel Paige. He'd say, "It's okay to look back, but just don't stare." When we come into anything new, such as a business, or a relationship, we have to remember we are going to have guilt. We have to make certain not to let that guilt eat us alive.

I still feel guilt today for being gone from Sarah while she was growing up. I go out today and cheer for her as she rides horses competitively, something she loves so dearly. That would never have been financially possible for a child of mine unless I made the sacrifices I made, but I still have difficulty shedding myself of that guilt. There is give and take in every situation.

We can't harbor guilt within us. It's the guilt of doing too well, the guilt of not doing well enough; it's the guilt that we should have treated someone differently, or that we shouldn't have said something to someone. As much as possible, we have to forget the past. I've heard it said, and believe it with all my heart— "Yesterday's history, tomorrow's a mystery, today is all we've got and it's a gift from God. That is why today is called the *present*."

When doors are closed in our lives I believe bigger doors open. Sometimes, though, if we become too comfortable in the room we are in, God has to give us a push out the door.

✳   ✳   ✳

Terry and Sandi Walker, National Sales Managers with Fortune, live in Arkansas. When I think of people who best represent the face of Fortune, Terry and Sandi always come to my mind. They are good, hard working individuals who have built a strong business with integrity, pure desire and a lot of "want to."

Terry and Sandi were Excel Representatives when that company closed its doors for good in 2004. I'm sure that was a very stressful time in their lives, not knowing how they would earn their next paycheck. But Terry and Sandi said to me, "Thank God Excel shut down because if it had not closed, we would have never come to Fortune and look what we would have missed." They are among the top earners in our company and they have reached that level by moving forward and taking advantage of the opportunity Fortune offers in the present.

I view Sheryl as a great example of remaining positive in the face of abrupt change. We married in November of 1999, and I guess there is no better way to break in a new marriage than to start a new company. We were in our second year of marriage and all of a sudden I took off my retirement mask and headed back into the work force. We basically went from doing a whole lot of nothing, to me reporting to work eight, nine hours a day.

If anyone could ever say this is not the life I signed up for, it is Sheryl. She supported Fortune and me 100% from day one; I feel so very fortunate. Now, neither of us can even imagine life without Fortune. It's like it has always been a part of our lives.

People are so busy planning their life, then it's over. Yet, they've spent all of their time planning. When I coached, I would say to my team, "We've been practicing, we've been working on drills, we've spent all this time rehearsing and now we're all dressed up with our pretty uniforms on—let's get out of this dadgum locker room and go play some ball."

I deliver a similar message to our Fortune Representatives, "You have been in there dressing, rehearsing, putting on your makeup, combing your hair, straightening your tie, fixing your skirt, polishing your shoes, putting on your earrings and you've been going through this same routine for fifteen years! It's time to get out there on the field and play the game. It's time to move beyond yesterday!"

One of the best quotes I ever read is from Frank Lloyd Wright, the famous architect of the late 19th and early 20th centuries. For more than seventy years, he designed impressive bridges, residential paradises, grand churches and monumental city buildings all over the world. He was asked toward the end of his life, "What is your best work of all time?" His answer was simply, "My next one!"

✳   ✳   ✳

THE MILLION DOLLAR TEST

Mʏ ʜɪɢʜ ꜱᴄʜᴏᴏʟ ʜᴏꜱᴛᴇᴅ ᴀ ʀᴇᴜɴɪᴏɴ in 2004 for our 1974 regional championship and state final-four baseball team. I wanted to attend so badly, but at the time I couldn't even get out of bed. My thoughts were of my friends returning to Boyle County, who didn't know how fortunate they were. I was never upset with anyone for their good health, but it just made me realize how many years I had taken for granted some of the most basic things in my life.

All those years I had been truly blessed, although I had never seen myself that way. I could run and exercise if I chose; at least I could always walk to the bathroom by myself. I'm not kidding, for the longest time when I was home in bed that was my greatest achievement of the day.

What price are we willing to pay to secure something that is really important to us?

I'm reminded of Steve Jordan from Oklahoma. He entered our business in November of 2004 and quickly earned the National Sales Manager position with Fortune. By the end of his first year he was doing exceptionally well. His income soared into the tens of thousands of dollars a month. Everything just fell into place for Steve and his wife, Shelly. Success in this business seemed to come easy to them, maybe too easy.

There can't be a testimony in life without a test! Those mountains we must climb, those obstacles we must overcome, that summit we want to reach, represent life's million dollar tests.

However, before long a series of tests dismantled their business. They experienced business deals that didn't pan out for them; their Fortune business income began to decline. Significantly! Their income had gone almost full circle. Additionally, they faced difficult personal challenges. Steve and Shelly didn't quit. They didn't say, "Well, we made it once but it must have been luck." They didn't listen to the people who said, "I told you it wouldn't last. Oh, I'm sure it could never happen again."

What price are *we* willing to pay to secure something that is really important to us?

What makes me so proud of Steve and Shelly is when their income went down, they went back to work. They solved their personal issues and cleaned up the business problems. They vowed to stay the course in order to get their income back on track. Against tough odds, they passed the test once again. To achieve that high level of income in your business, even once, is a tremendous feat that requires sacrifice and discipline; to do it twice is absolutely incredible.

We all face big tests in our lives. My battle with cancer was a million dollar test for me. Once I understood the nature of how cancer was able to survive in my body, I put into motion that inch-by-inch process to rid myself of the disease. By understanding and implementing the mandatory steps to keep it from returning to my body, I passed my million dollar cancer test.

There can't be a testimony in life without a test! Those mountains we must climb, those obstacles we must overcome, that summit we want to reach, represent life's million dollar tests. When we are faced with a million dollar test, guess what? In order to pass that test, we must respond with a million dollar answer.

In my experience with Excel I had more than one, million dollar test. In my opinion, Excel Representatives were led to believe by company leaders that the "Excel way" made us what we were. They thought if we left Excel or had never worked Excel, that we would never have been successful. I didn't believe that then, and I don't believe that now. I certainly don't believe our Fortune business is responsible for making our representatives successful.

Some of the Fortune Representatives I have highlighted such as Steve Jordan, Chris Doyle, Terry and Sandi Walker, Gilbert Anderson, and many more I haven't mentioned, are just mentally tough people. I believe their hard work and dedication, coupled with the help of the Fortune business, have brought them success. These people would be successful in any walk of life, if they chose to apply the same commitment they have in building their Fortune businesses.

They would lead successful lives with or without Fortune. They have paid a price over a period of months and years to get where they are. They all faced million dollar tests in their own personal lives as well as in their business lives. They have worked their way through those tests to earn the results they desired.

Certainly Abraham Lincoln faced the million dollar test in his life. He worked hard while growing up in Kentucky and Illinois. He educated himself and worked several jobs to pay his way through law school. Indeed, we are all too familiar with the story of the many setbacks and defeats that one of our nation's greatest leaders faced along the way. For example, he was defeated for Illinois State Representative in 1832; he lost his bid to Congress in 1843 then again in 1848; he campaigned for the nomination of Vice-President in 1856, but failed to make it onto his party's ticket; and he was defeated in his run for the United States Senate in 1858.

Abraham Lincoln lost eight times in his run for state and national offices. He also failed in business endeavors at least twice and suffered through a nervous breakdown before he was elected to any national office. Yet, through all these trials and tribulations, Lincoln remained focused to hold the country together. After each defeat he regrouped and refocused on his main objective. With his presidential victory in 1860, Lincoln was finally positioned to reach his ultimate goal. By staying the course and pressing through the many failures, Abraham Lincoln passed his test to the benefit of an entire nation. He was successful in fulfilling his passion to preserve the Union.

* * *

So often we fail to credit ourselves for the tests in our lives that we have successfully passed. My goodness, every single one of us has come through difficult struggles and come out better for it on the other side. The fact that Sarah and Jeffrey have turned out to be good young people is far more important than anything that I've accomplished financially in my life.

All of us have passed big tests in our lives that have had nothing to do with business matters. Our financial success doesn't have anything to do with whether or not we are great spouses. Financial success doesn't mean we are great spiritual leaders in our community. It doesn't mean we have stopped smoking or stopped gaining weight. If we have dedicated ourselves to improve our personal finances, that success doesn't address the other areas of our lives.

I was very unforgiving of myself during those first couple of years in Excel. My business wasn't progressing as fast as I thought it would. I had guilt. Man, I left a good job. Why did I leave a steady job? I had withdrawn and spent all my teacher retirement savings trying to stay afloat. I so wanted to just toss up my hands and say, "I quit; I'm outta here!"

I remember the Christmas of 1991 so clearly. Jeffrey and Sarah were at the age that they could tell if it was a good Christmas or not by the number of gifts around the tree. I didn't have an extra dollar to spend on presents because I had no idea how much money, if any, I was going to make on my next paycheck. Worst of all, at that time, I had passed judgment on myself. I felt like I was failing in every aspect of my life.

In 1992, I was about ten months into working my Excel business full-time, when I just pushed myself way too hard. I was burning the candle at both ends. I was barely making enough money to survive at that stage. I felt like the weight of the world was crashing down on me. I thought part of my job was to keep everybody in Excel happy and in my mind I became "Excel North" headquarters. I tried to fix everything for everybody in my business. People called me and said that their daddy's phone service hadn't been switched yet, or that their paycheck wasn't right for that month. Whether things are perceived to be real or whether they are real, it's just the same. If you think it, then you better believe it's real. My body responded by shutting down.

My first panic attack came while I was driving a car. For over a year after that I refused to get into a car by myself. Scrapper Letcher, a good friend of mine, always drove me to the places I needed to go. Then, I got to where I was okay getting into a car without someone else, but I wouldn't dare travel at night. I would make sure to arrive at my destination before sundown, stay overnight and leave the next morning. It was so embarrassing. People often asked me to join them for dinner after an evening meeting. I'd say, "No thanks," and head back to my room.

I weighed 230 pounds when my anxiety and panic attacks began and I was smoking three packs of cigarettes a day. No one asked me if I exercised, because it was pretty obvious that I didn't. Push-ups, sit-ups—no way. The thought of going out and running or jogging a mile would have made me pass out right where I stood. My physical self was dying.

One of my most embarrassing moments came when I went to speak at a meeting in Jackson, Mississippi. My neurologist had prescribed the medication Xanax for my anxiety attacks. After a brief rest, it was time to take my medication. I couldn't believe it! I had forgotten my Xanax in Danville. That realization triggered another panic attack.

Almost immediately there was a knock at my door. The two Excel members who arranged the meeting were standing there ready to show me to the conference room, but I was literally lying on the floor curled up like a baby. Thank goodness Scrapper was there. He assured them I'd be okay and I would be downstairs to speak in a few minutes. I did the meeting in a cold sweat.

I carried with me that garbage of guilt, pretending and hoping that nobody would find out that I was really no good at what I did. I thought I was supposed to be perfect and I was so miserably far from it. Fear, I've learned, is nothing more than premeditated failure. When we continue to agonize over a problem for a long period of time, we neglect to solve the problem. My neglect was that I refused to deal with those negative thoughts and feelings of failure, and the resulting guilt that followed. I allowed each problem to mushroom into an emergency, an end of the world scenario. I didn't know how to deal with the fear and the perceived pressure of the day to day issues that I faced.

Thomas Jefferson said, "There is no such thing as absolute freedom." That is exactly the dream I was chasing. I was pushing for that day when there would be no more responsibility. I was dreaming that financial success would make everything wonderful, and that I would have no more cares, no more worries. I was reaching for a kind of heaven on earth.

> *Fear, I've learned, is nothing more than premeditated failure.*

Finally, after beating myself up for the first few years as an Excel Representative, I allowed myself to remember achievements from the past and credit myself for those successes. My recollection of past struggles followed by successes helped me to erase my self-doubt and to put my life together again. Mostly, I began to understand that it was simply natural for everything in my life not to be perfect.

It's like the story of the boy walking down the street with his father. He tells his father that some day he wants to marry a beautiful woman, a smart woman, a wealthy woman who will make him happy for the rest of his life. His father looks down and says, "Son, make up your mind. We can't have it all."

Sure, we have to make sacrifices in various areas of our lives in order to achieve in other areas, but we have to emphasize the well-rounded view of life. We have to look at our health, our wealth, our spiritual life and our family life. We must try our best not to neglect any of these important aspects of our lives, and of course, to keep them in their proper perspective.

One very important thing that I have learned is that I'm not the general manager of the universe. I can't make everybody happy. What is the secret to happiness? I don't know, but I do know the secret to misery is trying to make sure everyone around you is happy. It just can't be done.

Now I realize there will never be a day when I'm not surprised about something. There will never be a day when I don't have a problem of some kind. Now I know that's okay. Things are never as bad as they seem, nor are they ever as good as they seem. I see the world a little differently today. I want to and strive to do my best, but like Art Williams advises in his book, "All you can do is all you can do." He goes on to say, "All you can do is enough."

✳   ✳   ✳

Billy Graham said when he was a young boy his father took him to a parade. Because of the crowd, there wasn't enough room to see. His dad put him on his shoulders so he could follow the parade through a knothole in the fence. All he saw was one segment of the parade at a time. The drummers went by, followed by the trumpet section. Next, Billy saw the baton girls, then the floats. Finally, the king and queen of the parade came into view, riding on the back of a convertible.

As an adult, it occurred to him that looking through that knothole is a lot like the view we have of life. Life is like a long parade, full of every instrument and many different kinds of floats. Basically, when asked how we are doing on any given day, our response depends on what we are seeing through the knothole. We must avoid basing our opinion of life merely on the narrow view provided through the knothole. We must see the entire parade for what it is. We must see how the different parts of the whole parade work together. We've got to get above the fence to see the real beauty of the parade.

We need to look at the bigger picture of our whole life and not just that knothole view of a single problem at the moment. Today's part of the parade may not be going too well, but maybe it will be different tomorrow when the drummers pass by.

When I have been able to rise above the fence and look at the entire parade of my life, I have passed my share of million dollar tests. With the good Lord's grace and the help of other people around me, my life has been better after the struggles. I am a better human being because of having had cancer. I am a better person because of having had anxiety attacks. I have learned one of life's important secrets: million dollar tests require million dollar solutions—AND when we pass life's BIG tests, we reap BIG rewards.

✳   ✳   ✳

SOME ASSEMBLY REQUIRED

ONE SPRING WHEN JEFFREY WAS ABOUT TWELVE, we went to Wal-Mart to look for him a new bicycle. There were dirt bikes, mountain bikes and ten-speeds, all kinds of bikes on display in the front of the store. Jeffrey was so excited. He walked back and forth and carefully viewed and reviewed the entire offering of bicycles. Finally, he said, "Dad, that one there! That's what I want." I thought, "Oh boy, I'm getting Jeffrey a bicycle today."

I removed the ticket from the bike and took it up to the counter. The cashier punched in the numbers and totaled up our purchase. She told us to pull around back to pick up the bike. I thought, "Man, this is going great!"

We drove around to the back of Wal-Mart and handed the employee our ticket. Jeffrey had a big smile on his face. We talked about showing that bike to his mom and how much fun it would be to ride it when we got home. Shortly, the person who took our ticket returned, and when he did, he was carrying a big box! I will never forget what was written in bold red letters on the side of that box: "SOME ASSEMBLY REQUIRED."

Oh, my gosh! Now there's work to do. Well, that's not exactly what I had in mind. I was so disappointed. I had the body of the bike, but it was not assembled. Before Jeffrey could enjoy the bicycle we had bought, I had to take the big box home, put on the wheels, put on the handlebars, attach the seat and essentially put the whole deal together.

Ruel Morton and Jerry Brown are giants in the Fortune business. When we attend a presentation and meet Ruel or Jerry, knowing they are ultra-successful, we ask, "Their paycheck is what? They're traveling where next week? They're donating how much, to whom? Oh yeah, that's what I'm signing up for; that's what I want."

Then, we become representatives of the company and we get our Fortune "box," our business kit. On the inside of the kit it says something to the effect of: "SOME ASSEMBLY REQUIRED."

Oh, my gosh! Now there's work to do. That's not exactly what I signed up for. Well, it's like Jeffrey's bicycle. Before we can enjoy the ride, there's work to be done.

Fortune Representatives are most vulnerable when they first enter our business. I know I was the most vulnerable when I started my Excel business. I had one foot in a dream world. I was thinking about the new world my family could have. I was dreaming of a better education for my children, of paying off the truck, of paying down the mortgage on our house or maybe completely paying off our home.

I still had one foot in the real world where people said I was crazy for getting involved with a network marketing company. Oh yeah, and the bills didn't stop coming just because I started dreaming. For me, as is the case for most of us, I was trying to replace my full-time financial nightmare with a part-time dream.

I remember coming home and saying to Carla, "Guess what I'm gonna do now, honey?" Of course, I had already told her that Tommy and I were going to make a bunch of money in real estate. I had already told her I was going to have paint crews running all over Danville. I had already told her I was going to lease more land and raise larger crops of tobacco to earn extra money. All of those projects had failed. So when I told her that I was going to do one more thing to supplement our income and that one thing was to work with a company called Excel, Carla basically responded with a, "Yeah, okay, fine," and rolled her eyes.

We need to understand those close to us really do want to believe us. But, most of the time, they don't pay a whole lot of attention to us because so many times before we've come home with the latest, greatest money-making idea that never seems to materialize. Excel was the fourteenth business idea I'd brought home in the last thirty days. Not literally, but that's what it sounds like to those who have heard it all before. Until we show that we can commit to something and stick with it, those who are closest to us are just going to roll their eyes and say, "Okay, here's just one more thing."

I've had people say to me, "I know working my own business is not going to be easy. I know I've got to get started. I know there are going to be tough tests along the way, but how do I make the business work? How do I go about assembling my own business?"

When I went full-time in Excel, I knew there was no turning back. I had no choice but to make it work. I've read before that pain is the only difference between knowledge and doing. For me pain is the link between knowing what to do and getting what you want to get done, done. I adopted a business strategy that I feel was very instrumental in my success. I made a decision to act and to do the things in my business I least wanted to do.

I've found that most of us know what we need to do in life, but most often it's the thing that we least want to do, that is the very next thing we need to do. We all know that we need to exercise regularly. We all know we need some kind of spiritual awareness. We all know if our personal finances are all screwed up. I was willing to learn and to take the necessary steps to achieve what I wanted to achieve.

Did I miss some good prospects? Oh, I'm sure I did, but I never allowed myself to be worn down by that constant drama of trying to convince someone else they needed to be working this business.

When I signed up to be an Excel representative on November 11, 1990, I didn't know how to build my business. On top of that, I hated the idea of having to ask people to try a new service or to even join a new company. The excitement of getting started, though, and the dreams I had to improve my family's quality of life, led me to take action.

I visited my good friend, David Camic, to ask him to try a new long distance service for me. I was so nervous as I walked up his sidewalk to knock on the door. I remember thinking, "The only thing worse than how I feel right now is being broke." I begged him for about an hour until he finally became a customer.

After he agreed, I walked back to my truck and helped him fill out the form to switch his long distance telephone service. I remember thinking to myself, "Orberson, you just did it. You're gonna be okay." The simple fact that I was willing to do something that I absolutely hated, showed me I had a fighting chance to do something big in this industry.

I didn't rent office space or spend a bunch of money on supplies in the early stages of my business. I tried my best to keep expenses down and I never attached my Excel business to a particular area.

Even though I never "opened up" a state, I allowed my business to follow its own natural progression. I traveled to wherever somebody who knew somebody, who knew somebody, would take me.

There is no foolproof plan to determine the best candidates for the network marketing industry. However, over the years I developed a three-step checklist that helped me: (1) I looked for "people, people." This group has an excitement for life. They are enthusiastic, energetic and enjoy getting out and meeting other people; (2) I sought people with credibility in their community; and (3) I looked for people who were in need of some additional income. By contrast, we could talk to Bill Gates's wife about earning an extra thousand dollars a month, but she probably wouldn't be too interested in the business.

I only took about twenty to thirty seconds to tell people what I was doing. If they didn't respond with a question about the Excel business, or if they didn't show any interest at all, I simply wouldn't talk about it any further. Did I miss some good prospects? Oh, I'm sure I did, but I never allowed myself to be worn down by that constant drama of trying to convince someone else they needed to be working this business. I learned by not begging and harassing, I saved my enthusiasm for the business and lived to fight another day.

Our perspective of the network marketing industry tends to be overly influenced by the attitude of the last person with whom we speak. We are on top of the world thinking this business is so great when we bring on a customer or sign someone into the business. However, if the next person we talk to doesn't want any part of the business, just like that, we question ourselves about what we are doing and we sit around and wonder why we ever started this crazy venture.

It's human nature to question why others don't see things the way we see them. We think everybody should fall down at our feet and sign up as soon as they hear about this great opportunity we've found.

Some people just miss it. Sometimes we go to the front door and there's nobody home, so we beat on the back door and, still, nobody's home. Then we get a stepladder and go to the back window and beat and beat and nobody's there either. Some people are simply not interested. Great, move on! Go to the next house.

Different businesses will take off at different times. Fortune Representatives like Steve and Miranda Bruce or Terry and Sandi Walker reached six-figure incomes their first year in the business. I was twenty-four months into my Excel business before I earned five figures for a month. I really never told anyone what my income was. If it was low, who would want to know that? If it was high, the number might seem out of reach for some people. I never wanted to discourage someone or make them feel like they had failed because they didn't make as much money as I did in a similar amount of time.

While I was with Excel, my income was always overestimated anyway. When I was making $1,000 a month, everyone said I was making $2,500 a month. When I made over $10,000 a month, they said I was making $20,000. By the time I actually made one million dollars in a month, most people talked like I had been making that much for many, many months.

We never know whether the words we are sharing are falling on rock or falling on fertile ground. When we introduce our business, we are not only talking to that person, but we are also talking to everybody that person knows. There were some nights when I presented the program or talked with someone about the business and came away thinking nobody was interested. I was down because I didn't sign anyone up that night, but I've learned the message those people may share with someone else can really help a business grow.

* * *

About three or four months into my Excel business, I was still coaching at Boyle County High School. I talked to Roscoe Denney, the basketball coach at Danville High School at the time, about the Excel opportunity. I said, "Roscoe, I've got something I think is really gonna be good here and I'd like you to sit down with me and take a look at it."

He said, "Nah, I'm not interested in looking at anything. I'm a coach!"

I said, "Okay," and I didn't talk with him about Excel for several weeks. After I started making a little money, I saw him again at the district tournament. I said, "Roscoe, there's more to life than this coaching stuff. I wish you'd take a look at this company I've been working with and what I've been doing over the last few months."

We never know whether the words we are sharing are falling on rock or falling on fertile ground.

Again, Roscoe answered, "I've already told you, Orberson, I'm not interested."

I said, "I understand," and left him alone.

A little over a year passed when I got home one evening and there was a phone message from guess who? Roscoe Denney. I remember his words, "Roscoe Denney here. I'm still not interested in that company you are working with, but I know the name of a man who I think would be good for you to talk with. It would be good for him and he just might be able to do something in your business. His name is Jim Voight." Well, you know how many times I'd heard that? I had taken down names like that a hundred times. Nothing had panned out much when I called people off of a suggestion from someone else. But I wrote down the name Jim Voight, along with his phone number, just as I had done with several other people I needed to call.

I didn't get around to calling Jim for a week or two, but when we talked he said he was definitely interested. We arranged to meet in Paducah, Kentucky, and I talked with him about the business. Jim signed up that night and I felt good about my trip. It was about a five hour drive home from Paducah and I stopped to call Roscoe on my way back to Danville. I said, "Roscoe, Jim Voight just signed up in Excel. You need to put your name in here as Jim's sponsor and let me sponsor you, because this guy says he's going to work the business and that could really benefit you."

I'll never forget Roscoe's response, "Buddy, I hope everything works out for you and Jim, I really do. But I've told you a hundred times, Orberson, I'm a coach and that's all I want to do."

Never underestimate the potential of what you view as bad days to turn into really good days. Initially, Roscoe Denney turned me down. I thought I had received a final rejection that night at the district basketball tournament, and although Roscoe said no, I did talk with him about the business. While Roscoe made it clear that he was not interested in my business, the message he left on my answering machine served as the catalyst to forever change my life.

I didn't think the phone call to Jim would produce anything positive. I really did not want to make that trip to Paducah to meet with Jim Voight, but I did what I didn't want to do. Jim quit his teaching and coaching position after he had been in Excel for only two weeks and I was scared to death for him. Like myself, Jim was not a likely candidate to be successful in business. He had no particular background for the business world. But he was another one of those individuals who had so much "want to" that he would not be denied. He worked his business hard for about four years and made a bunch of money. In fact, Jim Voight went on to become the second leading money earner in the Excel company.

Every time I presented the program or talked to someone about Excel, I thought about Roscoe and Jim. The person I was talking to may not be interested, but someone they knew just might! I was ready all the time! I tried my best to make every trip. I was always afraid if there was a trip I didn't make, I would miss out on another "Jim Voight."

I've learned so much over the years in the network marketing industry. Certainly my experiences have been great teachers, but I have made many, many great friends and have been associated with representatives along the way who have helped shape my view of the industry today.

Betty Miles always comes to mind when I think of lessons I've learned by watching other people work in this industry. I've heard her say so many times that what makes network marketing work is people caring about people. Betty is from South Carolina and was very successful in the insurance business before she started in Excel in the 1990's.

I love to hear her talk about corporate America and the fighting, clawing and scratching that goes on among people striving to reach the top. Many individuals believe the goal in corporate America is to climb over as many people as they can in order to get that promotion. Unfortunately, they seem to be in constant competition with their "partners" in the office and do not hesitate to lower anyone else in order to raise themselves.

Betty earned over one million dollars in just her second year with Excel, and was in the top ten money earners of the entire company. Today, as a Fortune Representative, she has become such a strong leader and example of how to build a successful business in the right way. She puts into practice what she teaches. In network marketing our goal is to elevate, uplift and help as many people as possible. The only way for our business to grow is to help someone else in this business succeed.

When Betty first started in this industry, she worked with a lot of women on welfare who had no other way to take care of themselves except through the government. She was able to help many of them become successful in their businesses and become financially independent.

> *"When you do the common things in life in an uncommon way, you will command the attention of the world."*
> *—George Washington Carver*

I know this was more rewarding for Betty than the money she made. I think she was born to serve other people and help them have hope for the future.

The network marketing business is not rocket science. George Washington Carver said, "When you do the common things in life in an uncommon way, you will command the attention of the world." It's doing the simple things and applying the discipline to get things done that builds a successful business.

There's no question about the fact that it takes work. But work is good! Work is Scripture. We can't be afraid of work. I always tell the story about the salesman who says to a customer, "This machine will cut your work in half."

The customer says back to the salesman, "Great, I'll take two."

Most people do only what they are required to do, but successful people do a little bit more, and in some cases a lot more. Good things come to those who go after what the other fellow sits back and waits for. As we assemble our business, we must do today what others will not do, so that we may have tomorrow what others will not have.

✳   ✳   ✳

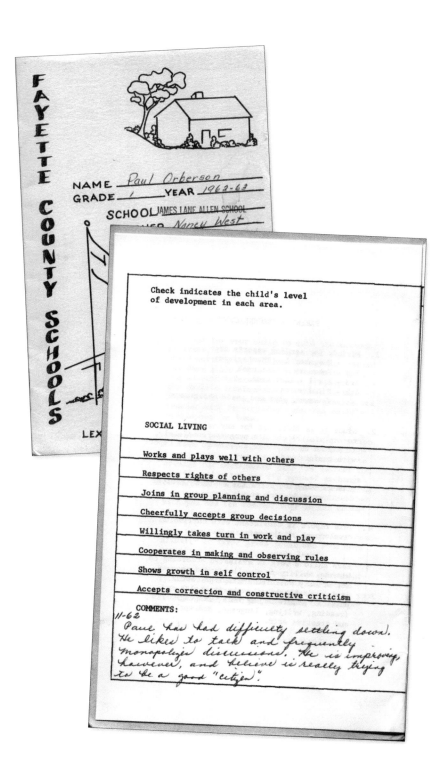

FAYETTE COUNTY SCHOOLS

NAME _Paul Orberson_
GRADE _1_ YEAR _1962-63_
SCHOOL JAMES LANE ALLEN SCHOOL
TEACHER _Nancy West_

LEX

Check indicates the child's level
of development in each area.

SOCIAL LIVING

Works and plays well with others

Respects rights of others

Joins in group planning and discussion

Cheerfully accepts group decisions

Willingly takes turn in work and play

Cooperates in making and observing rules

Shows growth in self control

Accepts correction and constructive criticism

COMMENTS:
11-62
Paul has had difficulty settling down.
He liked to talk and frequently
monopolizes discussions. He is improving,
however, and believe is really trying
to be a good "citizen".

Orberson Pitches No-Hitter, Boyle Wins

Beldon Bangs Three Triples, Rebels Advance Into Finals

By BILL VAUGHT
Sports Editor

Paul Orberson fired a no-hitter and Joe Beldon slammed three triples to spark the Boyle County Rebels to a 7-2 victory over Franklin County Friday afternoon at Shively Sports Center on the University of Kentucky campus in Lexington.

The win came in the Regional tourney semi-finals and moved the Rebels into the title game against Tates Creek. The championship game is set for Tuesday afternoon at 4:00 at Shively Sports Center. The winner will advance to the state tournament which will be played at Morehead University.

Orberson, Boyle's ace hurler, now shows an 8-1 season record, breezed through the first six innings of the game with no problems as Franklin had only three base runners and only one man had reached second base. However, according to Paul he began to tire about the no-hitter in the sixth inning.

Realizing that he had a no-hitter going in his grasp Orberson obviously began to work harder and faster in the seventh inning. The combination of four walks

first baseman Greg Wilson had possession of the ball on the bag and was watching the runner at third when he was run into by the Franklin base runner which resulted in his dropping the ball and the runner was called safe.

Joe Beldon, Dallas Pennington and Paul Orberson provided most of the offensive punch for the Rebels. Beldon had a great day while whacking three triples in as many times at bat. Beldon's third three-bagger came in the sixth inning and was hit straight toward the 400-foot sign in direct center field. The ball carried over the Franklin center fielder's head and he scored three times. He was credited with four runs batted in.

Dallas Pennington, Boyle's fleet-footed center fielder, also had a fine day. Dallas was credited with two hits and beat out an infield ground ball that could have been ruled a third hit. He stole second all three times he reached first and he also scored three times. He scored once from second on an infield ground ball that was fielded and thrown high to first. The Franklin first baseman handled the ball after a high

JOE BELDON is shown above coming into third base after stroking his third triple during Regional tourney game in Lexington. Joe's bat was a key factor in Boyle High's 7-2 win over Franklin County. The baseball is seen at center of photo as Franklin third baseman and umpire [...] are shown at right of photo.

Orberson Does His Thing Again . . .

Rebels Are Regional Champs - Now In State

By BILL VAUGHT
Sports Editor

[...] of the brightest moments [...] Boyle County High School's [...] history came yesterday [...] in Lexington when the [...] won the Regional [...] tourney championship [...] cinching a 4-1 victory [...] Creek's Commodores in [...] title game advanced Boyle [...] next week's state high [...] tourney which will be [...] at Morehead University. [...] Rebels of Coach Bob Gorley [...] now among the final eight [...] teams in Kentucky.

[...] Orberson, the Rebels [...] left-handed hurler, did his [...] beautifully again [...] and was never in [...] serious trouble except for a [...] loaded situation in the [...] inning. Paul yielded only [...] hits to the Lexington team [...] one of them was a bunt [...] to the third which was the [...] Tates Creek hit will [...] [...] inning. [...] Orberson struck out three [...] walked only two [...] going the full seven, in [...] inning.

[...] [Orberson] across they made

when his slow hit ground ball was over thrown at first. Paul Orberson drew a walk and stole second.

John Joe Beldon then came through again for the Rebs as he delivered a two-run single and the Boyle team had the early 3-0 edge. From this point on the game was a real pitching battle between Orberson and Jervis of TC.

The turning point in the game could well have been the second

Rebs Play State Game On Tuesday

The State High School baseball tournament will be played at Morehead State University's Allen Field and will open on Monday. June 5 and continue through Thursday, June 8. The Boyle team Rebels are scheduled to meet Paducah-Tilghman at 1:30 o'clock Tuesday, June 6. The first game at 3:30 Tuesday will match Elizabethtown against a Holy Cross. Winners meet

inning when Tates Creek loaded the bases with only one out. A base single, an error and a walk filled the sacks. But Orberson met the challenge and struck out the next batter before the third out came on a fly ball to right field. Getting out of the jam appeared to lift both Orberson and his teammates.

Tension mounted with the passing of each inning and going into the sixth the Rebs were still clinging to the 3-0 lead. The pressure was eased somewhat when the Rebels added a run in the sixth for a 4-0 bulge. Mike Orberson singled and stole second. He then scored on a Roger Webb single.

Tates Creek managed to get only its second hit in the bottom of the sixth but it went for naught as Orberson remained tough. Orberson then aided his cause in the top of the seventh when his double drove in Vaskey who had walked and single scored. Tension was eased running extremely high by this time, and the insurance run again eased nerves a little.

Several Boyle County fans were in attendance at yesterday's game and they were on the edge of their seats as the last of seventh got underway. Creek caused a new

seven hits with Joe Beldon and catcher Tommy Hellon, who turned in a fine effort, getting two singles each. Other hitters were Paul Orberson with a double, Mike Orberson and Roger Webb had singles. The Rebs showed three stolen bases in the game and all three steals led to runs being scored.

Coach Bob Gorley was extremely pleased following the game stated, "I thought our kids turned in a great effort out there today and this is what we've been pointing for all season."

Dedicated Win To Joe Robinson

The Rebels dedicated the victory to former Rebel manager Joe Robinson who is one of the team's most avid fans. Joe has attended many of the Rebel's games this season but was unable to make the trip yesterday since he had to work. We doubt that anybody was much happier than Joe when he heard the report on yesterday's game.

Scouts Were At The Game

Big league baseball scouts representing the St. Louis Cardinals and San Francisco Giants were in attendance for [...] national finals at [...]

HAPPY REBELS—Following the last out in yesterday's Regional tourney title game the Boyle County Rebels were a jubilant group. In the photo above winning pitcher Paul Orberson (center) is being congratulated by teammate Jerry Hilbert.

Dallas Pennington walk left while Mike Orberson with a big smile on his face defeated Tates Creek 4 [...] tournament.

Boyle's 'Mr. Everything'

Orberson stars on mound and elsewhere for 19-0 team

By DON SNIDER
Courier-Journal & Times Staff Writer

Good baseball players come from most anywhere in Kentucky.

The Cincinnati Reds' Don Gullet is from Lynn, Ky. The Minnesota Twins' Phil Roof hails from Paducah. Woodie Fryman of the Detroit Tigers calls Ewing home, while Denny Doyle is the pride of the California Angels from Horse Cave.

Then there's Paul Orberson. Paul who? Orberson isn't in the same class with those major leaguers. But folks in Boyle County say he's in a high school class of his own.

Boyle County High owes much of its 19-0 record to Orberson, a left-handed senior who has pitched six of those victories and played wherever needed in the others.

"We've had good players around here," says Boyle County's Bob Gorley, who's been coaching at the school six years, "but I think Paul's the best I've seen. He's by far our best pitcher. He pitches against the toughest teams and he's had three shutouts and allowed only two earned runs."

Orberson's statistics don't mean much, however. If Boyle County didn't overwhelm so many opponents, he would see a lot more mound action. Monday, for example, Boyle County crushed Waynesburg Memorial 20-3, scoring 12 runs before there were any outs. The Boyle County starters played only the first inning.

But Orberson, says his coach, "wants to play all the time."

So when he's not placed [...] he'll sit out in

center field or playing short unusual (for a southpaw) spots as third base. Orberson also is batting .444 and has stolen 30 bases ("I don't think he's been thrown out once," says Gorley).

Naturally, a lot of scouts have their eye on Paul, the son of a Danville minister and an all-around athlete who was the school's leading scorer as a wide receiver in football and has run the dashes on the track team and played some varsity basketball.

"He'll probably go to college," says Gorley. Several Ohio Valley Conference schools have shown interest. He'd make a good college outfielder or pitcher. But a pro career would depend on how he grows.

"He's strong and wiry (5-11, 155

pounds)," said Gorley, "but as a pro he would need a little more weight and maturing. He's only 17 years old."

In the meantime, Orberson is concentrating on getting Boyle County into the state high school tourney finals which are June 3-6 at Morehead. Last year, Boyle County could beat everybody but Henry Clay in 28 games, losing twice to the Lexington school, the last time in the regional. Henry Clay went on to win the state title.

Orberson is complemented by his brother, Mike, 16, a junior second baseman hitting over .400, and catcher-infielder Mike Brummett, pitcher-infielder Joe Beldon and outfielders Dallas Pennington and Roger Webb, all batting between .350 and .400.

Boyle County steals at every opportunity. Last year, the team swiped 210 bases in 28 games (by contrast, Cincinnati led the majors with 148 in 162 games) and once stole 20 bases in a 15-2 victory over Casey County.

But to keep the school out of the state tourney this year, somebody might have to "steal" Paul Orberson from the lineup.

Late Monday box score

Yankees 6, Rangers 4

NEW YORK / TEXAS box score

Monday's ABA playoff box

AT UTAH (132)—Jones 32, Beaty 27, Wise 29, Mount 19, Govan 6, Boone 2, Watson 2, Beasley 1, Sears 0.

NEW YORK (133)—Taylor 15, Williamson 14, Dale 11, Ladner 2, Netolicky [...]

Attendance—10,742.

That's me, just
getting started.
1957

My hero, Grandpa
Garry, holding me
in his backyard on
Chestnut Street.
Danville, Kentucky, 1957

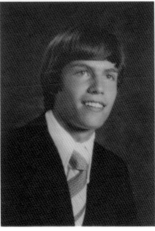

5th Grade,
Perryville
Elementary.
My teeth are
bigger than
my head!
1967

Senior, Boyle
County High
School
1974

College Years:
Standing with
Jeff in front of our
trailer, Lot # 28,
Skyline Trailer Park,
Bowling Green,
Kentucky.
1975

Carla and Jeff, with
me, on graduation day,
Western Kentucky
University.
1979

Doing my baseball
coaching thing at Casey
County High School.
Spring, 1981

Tommy and his wife, Alane—we're headed to a dinner cruise in Seattle, Washington. This picture was taken during my bad habit days—smoking one, with plenty more in my other hand.
1993

My first riding mower. Sarah loved it! There were times when we even cut some grass while we were out riding around.
1991

Excel meeting, Louisville
1992

Quiet reflection.
2007

Ed and Sheila
Orberson, my
father and mother.
2000

Wedding day for Jeff—
I'm the proud daddy.
September, 2002

Sheryl and I enjoy a night out in Cincinnati, catching a Reds' game at The Great American Ballpark. *Summer, 2007*

Sarah jumping
in a horse show.
Summer, 2002

Donald McGhee (front left), and Barry Levy (right) working on food boxes for the FHTM Foundation. *2007*

After years of public speaking, I have finally overcome my fear. *Summer, 2007*

Sometimes lunch or breakfast, sometimes I just bring candy—the office staff always seems happy to see me! *2007*

Ring of Honor inductees. *Summer, 2007*

Early morning
push-ups at
the office.
2007

Seated with Fortune
Representatives
Kathy Taylor (middle)
and Monna Lane
discussing new
product information.
2007

Tommy and I find time to laugh, most of the time at each other. *2007*

At the home office in Lexington, Kentucky, with Tommy and Jeffrey. *2007*

The Fortune staff—a great group of people. They are always willing to do whatever it takes to get the job done. I appreciate them so much! *2007*

Orberson Has WKU Records

"Records are nice but winning the conference is the most important thing to me right now."

Those words of wisdom were uttered by Paul Orberson, a 1974 graduate of Boyle County High School, Tuesday when he was contacted at his residence in Bowling Green.

The Western Kentucky University senior pitcher is having a super season for the Hilltopper baseball team and Monday was the winner in a 4-2 triumph over the University of Kentucky. He went six innings and allowed only four hits while striking out six.

That victory improved his individual record to 6-3 and tied a Western record for most wins in one season (Orberson now shares the record with Donnie Durham of Casey County). In addition, the southpaw has now worked 62 innings and that establishes a new WKU mark.

Western has already won its division of the Ohio Valley Conference and will meet East Tennessee on May 5 and 6 for the conference crown. The best two-out-of-three series will determine which school represents the OVC in the NCAA Tournament in Miami, Fla.

Orberson tells, "We are all working to winning the conference right now. That is our primary objective. Individual records are nice but they don't mean near as much as winning the OVC."

Still, the modest lefthander has compiled some impressive individual stats this year. His earned run average is now under 1.5 as he has yielded only 14 earned runs in 62 innings. He is throwing harder than ever and tells, "Right now I am throwing as good as I have ever thrown in my life."

Bob Gorley, his high school coach, saw him throw at UK Monday and said, "He was in total control of the game. The one run they did get came on an excuse-me type of hit. Paul just had too much stuff for them."

Even Paul had to admit that he had a good day. He laughed, "They were just popping the ball up or grounding out. I only planned to go five innings because I am going to pitch again Thursday. But after five I had thrown so few pitches that I went ahead and worked the sixth. I only threw 62 pitches all afternoon."

Orberson will be eligible for the June major league draft but he doesn't know if he has a chance to be picked by a big league team or not. He recalled, "When we played at Miami in March they had scouts lined up all over the field. It was my first game and when I went out after seven we were leading 2-1. We lost 3-2 but they were ranked third in the country."

The former Rebel feels like getting to play in the NCAA tourney would boost his chances of getting drafted. And to hear Orberson talk there is little chance of Western losing the OVC crown. He explained, "I don't want it to sound like I am bragging but I just don't think a team can come in here and beat us twice."

Paul is hoping that he will be drafted because he would like a crack at professional baseball. But if he isn't chosen he will be able to accept that.

Everybody predicted Orberson would make a fine college hurler. Well, everybody did except UK coach Tuffy Horne. And now maybe even Horne will admit that Orberson can pitch.

Good luck to Paul in the OVC playoffs and we certainly hope that he is taken in the June draft.

Paul Orberson

UK
UNIVERSITY
OF KENTUCKY
ATHLETICS

Athletics Association

Memorial Coliseum
Lexington, Kentucky 40506-0019

UK ATHLETICS MEDIA RELATIONS
For Immediate Release: January 7, 1999

GENEROUS DONATION TO HELP BUILD NEW UK FOOTBALL OFFICES

A $1.6-million dollar pledge from former Kentuckian Paul Orberson will be used in the construction of a new football office complex at the University of Kentucky's Nutter Training Center, UK Athletics Director C.M. Newton has announced.

The offices for Coach Hal Mumme and the football staff are currently located in Commonwealth Stadium. The new complex will enable Coach Mumme and his staff to be more accessible to the players. In addition, having the coaches in the same building as the video office, training room, weight room and equipment room will improve the efficiency of the staff.

Orberson, a native of Boyle County and a 1974 graduate of Boyle County High School, is a lifetime UK sports fan who attended Western Kentucky University on a baseball scholarship. After graduation, Orberson returned to Boyle County High School as a teacher and baseball coach. He joined Excel Communications in a part-time capacity in 1989 and retired from coaching and teaching to devote himself full-time to the company in 1991. Orberson's enormous success enabled him to retire from the company in 1996 and he is now a major stockholder in Teleglobe Corporation, which purchased Excel. Teleglobe is the fourth-largest long distance carrier in the country and the second-largest internet infrastructure in the world.

Orberson, who now resides in Florida, has two children – Jeff, who attends Eastern Kentucky University, and Sarah, who is a student at Lexington Christian Academy.

"We want to express our deepest gratitude to Paul and his family for helping us continue toward our goal of making our football program one of the nation's best in all areas," Newton said.

-UK-

UKFootball

■ DONATION

Gift will pay for football offices

By Mark Story
HERALD-LEADER STAFF WRITER

A guy who made millions selling long-distance for Excel Telecommunications Inc. is going to foot the bill for a new office complex for the University of Kentucky football coaches.

Paul Orberson, formerly of Danville, will donate $1.6 million, UK Athletics Director C.M. Newton announced yesterday, all of which will go toward the construction of new offices for Coach Hal Mumme and his staff.

The office complex will be built at the Nutter Training Center, which currently houses the dressing rooms and weight lifting facilities for the UK football players.

(That facility should not be confused with the Nutter Field House, an indoor training facility which features a football field inside).

Newton said the plans for the office complex have not been submitted to the state for approval so there is no official starting date for the project.

The UK Board of Trustees and the UK Athletics Association Board also must approve the donation.

The football coaching offices are currently at Commonwealth Stadium. Newton said the school would probably move the offices for coaches of other sports into the space that will be vacated by football.

He said Orberson's donation will pay for the whole project.

Orberson played college baseball at Western Kentucky University and is a former boys' basketball coach at Boyle County High School. He became a millionaire as an independent sales representative for Excel Telecommunications Inc.

That company marketed long-distance telephone service via a multi-level marketing system.

Orberson, who went to work for Excel part-time in 1989 and full-time in 1991, was the most successful salesman in the company's history.

He retired in 1996 and is now a major stockholder in Teleglobe Corp., which purchased Excel.

Asked why he chose to make such a sizable donation, Orberson said "I know they really need this and I've got more (money) than I need."

He said he first began having talks about making the donation with UK associate athletics director Kathy DeBoer last year. This year, Orberson said he has dealt primarily with new assistant AD Alvis Johnson, the former Harrodsburg High School football coach.

The pair knew each other when both were high school coaches.

"Coach Johnson and I got to where we were meeting every week or two," Orberson said. "And Larry Vaught sort of put

"I know they really need this and I've got more (money) than I need."

Paul Orberson,
who donated
$1.6 million for a
new office
complex

this thing together. He sort of got me together with Alvis."

Vaught, the sports editor of the Danville Advocate-Messenger, said his role was persuading UK that Orberson had the wherewithal to make a substantial donation.

"I don't think UK was taking him seriously," Vaught said. "I knew he had the money and I knew he was very sincere in wanting to give it. I just was in a position to tell them 'Hey, you need to pay this guy some attention.'"

COMPETING FOR THE NATIONAL TITLE

AN OLD FRENCH PROVERB SUGGESTS that in the beginning everything is wonderful, and it's true. In the beginning of a new project, job or business, everything looks great. We have dreams fresh in our minds and our enthusiasm is high. We are excited about all the endless possibilities for the future.

Then somewhere along the way, in a few weeks or a few months, we hit the middle stage of our new endeavor. I call it the middle mile. It's that middle mile that wears us down. We don't see ourselves close enough to the finish line, yet we've gone beyond that starting point where the beginning was fresh and we were inspired to get up and get going. The middle mile links the beginning to the end. We all know we have to endure it. It is the most dangerous time in any undertaking, when quitting looks awfully good.

I've been good at starting things all my life. I started Cub Scouts when I was in grade school. We bought the blue uniform and the little blue hat, but I didn't stick with it. Later, I thought it would be cool to play the violin. We found a used violin and a teacher; I took a few lessons, but I quit. I wanted to play the guitar when I became a high school student. I pictured myself on stage playing in front of large crowds in huge arenas. I took a few lessons, then I quit. Prior to my Excel business, it seemed that starting something new was easy. It was holding on through that middle mile that was always the toughest for me.

I went to the front desk and handed the hotel clerk my Visa card to pay for a room. The card was rejected! Well, okay. I pulled out my MasterCard. The clerk said, "This one has been denied, too. I'm sorry."

In July of 1992 I wasn't generating enough money to make a living in my Excel business. I was driving my Nissan pickup truck all over God's creation trying to generate more income. One night I drove to Huntington, West Virginia, for a meeting at the Holiday Inn. There were a few representatives there who were already in the business, but no new prospects. It seemed to be another dry run. I just wanted to get a room and get some sleep after the meeting. I had been on the road for six or seven days a week for the past several weeks and I was absolutely worn out. I went to the front desk and handed the hotel clerk my Visa card to pay for a room. The card was rejected! Well, okay. I pulled out my MasterCard. The clerk said, "This one has been denied, too. I'm sorry." I was at the point where I had spent all of my money to keep the business afloat. I had maxed out all of my credit cards and I just stood there staring at the floor. I'm sure I looked like a beat up pup. I know that's how I felt.

Of course I was embarrassed. Of course I was frustrated. My only option was to get back in my truck. I left Huntington late that night. I was so tired. I pulled over at a rest area just inside the Kentucky border and fell asleep in my truck. A couple of hours later, I woke up and headed for home. I was still exhausted; I was tired of network marketing. I was tired of living in my truck. I was tired of getting farther and farther behind with my house and truck payments. I was tired of bills, bills of every kind that kept piling up. My business was simply not growing as fast as I had hoped. My dreams were fading right before my eyes.

All the way home, all I could think about was how I was going to tactfully quit my Excel business. How was I going to tell people that I just couldn't do it anymore? How was I going to tell my family? Before I reached home, though, I remembered a powerful message I had read: "When you get so tired that you think about giving up or quitting what you are doing, think about looking your youngest child in the eye and saying, 'I don't have the courage to win for you.'" That thought stuck with me, ringing and ringing in my ears.

I thought, "How can an average, ordinary person raised in an average, ordinary home like mine, win for my family?" Heck, I love my family as much as professional sports figures do. I want to help out in my community as much as they do. What about me? I know I don't have the skills of great athletes. I can't go into training and come out 6'9" tall. I can't run a 4.3 forty-yard dash and play in the National Football League. I can't throw a baseball ninety-five miles per hour. How can an average, ordinary person like me compete for a national title for my family?

Yes, I was tired. Yes, I was frustrated. Yes, I wanted to give in, give up and I was ready to give out. By the time I got home, I couldn't tell Sarah that I was quitting on her. I couldn't tell her that I couldn't win for her. I realized the only way someone like me could win big financially for my family was to stick with network marketing and to continue my Excel business.

I spent some quality time with Sarah and Jeffrey that morning. Then, I made some phone calls to members of my organization, set up some more speaking engagements and jumped right back into my business, full throttle.

That experience taught me a great lesson in responsibility. I was accountable to someone. My purpose in life was much bigger than myself. I really believe we all must be accountable to someone. We must be accountable to our families, or our church, or our charitable mission. We must stand up and be willing to give an account of ourselves whatever our purpose may be.

There are adults who would prefer Little League baseball games to be played without even keeping score, so we don't hurt anybody's feelings. I'm sorry, that's not the way life works. I know winning isn't everything. I'm not even saying that winning is necessarily the most important thing. But to play the game of Little League baseball without keeping the score is equivalent to playing the "financial game" in life without planning for retirement, without having a family emergency fund, without having a college tuition plan for your children, without knowing your home mortgage rate or the length of time it will take to pay it off. Yet, that is exactly what most of us do in our adult lives.

We are all players in the "financial game of life." There is no doubt we are participating, whether we admit it to ourselves or not. Most of us play the game without even knowing what inning it is. We are no closer to the fifth inning or to the sixth inning than we were ten years ago. We don't have any idea how many outs there are and we have no earthly idea what the score is—other than it ain't good! Most of us are so far behind that we think if we score just a single run, it will keep us in the game for another month or two.

We don't need to keep score just for the sake of keeping score, but understanding how we are positioned in our financial lives allows us to show some accountability for who we are and where we are going. Make no mistake about it, there are innings and there is a certain number of outs. We only have "X" amount of time. I've learned through experiences with my grandfather when I was in high school, and from the automobile accident I had the night of his funeral, that life is short. Life on this earth ain't forever.

If your financial purpose in life does not include network marketing, that's okay. But man, get yourself a purpose. Live life with purpose! There is more to us being here than just breathing and taking up space. If you're not living life on the edge, then you're taking up too much space.

This business is not about how much we want it. It's really not. It's about how long we want it. We don't need any special talent or skills to succeed in network marketing, just the desire. Hall of Fame football coach George Allen said, "People of mediocre ability sometimes achieve outstanding success because they don't know when to quit. Most men succeed because they are determined to." Success is all about "want to."

People sometimes admit to me that they are close to quitting. I know there comes a time in all endeavors when quitting looks good. In marriage, college, relationships and jobs, thoughts of quitting are perfectly normal. When I run on a treadmill, I dream of quitting the whole time. I dream of pushing that stop button. Sheryl often says the difference between her and me is that I enjoy exercising. Wrong! I enjoy it when it's over.

Joe B. Hall, the former basketball coach at the University of Kentucky, told the Wildcats, "We will have fun when the season is over and we have won the National Championship. Until then it's not going to be much fun." I don't like to get on the treadmill, but I get over it. It's gonna happen. I'm gonna do it. No use trying to talk myself out of it. I hate it. I really do. I hate doing push-ups and sit-ups every day, curling weights and lifting them over my head. I hate that junk, but I know I've got so many push-ups I need to do, so many sit-ups I need to do and a certain distance I need to run, so I just do it. Yes, I do enjoy finishing the workout, but I don't relish the thought of the actual workout.

✳   ✳   ✳

We struggled in the first few months of our Fortune business, but I knew, short of a nuclear war, Tommy and I weren't going to quit. We were committed and truly believed in this business from day one. Our business model was strong. However, it takes some time for the outside world to believe in you as a company. There have been so many network marketing companies that have started and failed. Many people just couldn't imagine that our business would succeed as a legitimate marketing company for the long haul.

Tommy and I were desperately seeking leadership from our representatives at that time and we were looking for someone to take the bull by the horns and provide some stability to the Fortune program. That's when I met Todd Rowland at a breakfast meeting in Little Rock, Arkansas. Todd became a Fortune Representative in the first year of our company and certainly provided the much needed leadership Fortune was seeking. He was also instrumental in the early growth of our Fortune business. He wasn't appointed leader; he appointed himself leader.

A winner throughout his ten-year coaching career, Todd Rowland had worked his way into his dream job in the fall of 2000. He was a high school football coach at 5A powerhouse, Fort Smith Northside, in Arkansas. His wife, Ashley, had just given birth to their third child.

They made the decision for her to leave her job so she could stay home with the kids and manage the homefront. Although Todd loved coaching and teaching, he found himself having to do odd jobs on the side just to keep up with the financial demands of his growing family. Between coaching, teaching and the time he spent with part-time jobs, Todd was working around the clock.

In 2001, Todd was invited to a Fortune meeting by his father and decided the program made a lot of sense. He and Ashley prayed about the business opportunity, and Todd believes his Fortune business was an answer to those prayers. Coming up with the $299 wasn't easy. Fortunately, Todd's father stepped up and provided Todd and Ashley with the money to invest in themselves to become Fortune business owners. They were certain the business would be the perfect vehicle to provide them with some much needed extra income. Unfortunately, they soon realized everyone was not as eager as they were to get involved with the business.

There were nine coaches on the staff at Fort Smith. After Todd signed on with Fortune, he returned to them to share the business opportunity. Each coach had a desk of his own in a huge office where they watched films and designed game plans on a big, dry-erase board. On this particular day, Todd wrote on the board in the coaches' office that he had just signed up in the Fortune business and wanted to show the coaches the program. Their reaction was not what Todd had anticipated. Not one of the coaches on that staff ever joined. One of the coaches had been on staff for thirty-four years. He didn't necessarily enjoy his job, but financially, he couldn't afford to quit. He told Todd, "That kind of stuff ain't ever going to work. You've got one of the best jobs in the state. Why are you wanting to mess around with all that stuff?" Todd realized at that moment that he never wanted to be locked into a job that he didn't like, unable to retire simply because he had to have the income.

Did Todd have doubts whether Fortune Hi-Tech Marketing was the vehicle to take him where he wanted to go financially with his life? I'm sure he did! We all have those thoughts of doubt. Doubt is perfectly normal, yet I've found that winners act in spite of doubt. We are not always going to be full of faith, but winners act in spite of their lack of faith. There are times when we may feel more married than others, but make no mistake about it, we are still married. There are times when we feel like we are better parents, and times, perhaps, when we feel like we haven't been as good of a parent as we should. That doesn't make us any less of a parent. We are still parents. Certainly, there are times when our commitment to different parts of our lives waivers, including our commitment to our financial lives. That doesn't mean we give up and walk away from it. The best thing to do when we overeat is not to give up on a healthy diet or give up on the whole program, but to return to the healthy lifestyle the next day.

Doubts can be overcome when we hold on to that constant feeling that no matter the current circumstance, something good's gonna happen in our life. Some people might say that's Pollyannaish and doesn't work. To me, it's the only way to think. Believe in the power of positive thinking. It is suspected that the diagnosis of cancer kills more people than the cancer itself. Abraham Lincoln professed, "People are about as happy as they make up their mind to be." I believe that's true.

Todd presented the Fortune opportunity to his closest working partners but none of them joined him. He didn't quit. He pressed on. About four months into the business, he was standing in the lunchroom when his principal, Dr. Barry Owen, asked about his business. Todd told him he was making a couple of hundred dollars each month and it was going pretty well. Todd asked him to take a look at the business.

That night Todd went to Dr. Owen's house and explained the business to him and his wife. They signed up on the spot. A few days later, Dr. Owen encouraged a couple of history teachers to join. One of those teachers signed up a relative, who signed up a fireman, who signed up another fireman, Scott Grizzle. Scott took off immediately with his business. He brought an orthodontist into the business and he got rolling with a great start. That occurrence of seemingly unlikely events, skyrocketed Todd's paycheck from $400 to $6,800 in ninety days. But then again, that's exactly how network marketing works!

Todd's business exploded. His $6,800 check for one month was over twice what he was bringing home from the school system where he had ten years experience and a master's degree. Todd and Ashley made the decision to go full-time. Their business continued to prosper as they began their second year in the company. They earned their first monthly check in excess of $30,000 in their nineteenth month with Fortune. That amount was close to matching his entire yearly income as a teacher and coach.

Sometimes people don't take network marketing as a serious business or career possibility. For Todd and Ashley, their Fortune business is their career opportunity. Todd works his business just like any other legitimate one. They work hard. I've heard Todd say, "If you are going to be successful, you have to have total faith in what you are doing."

Todd consistently earns hundreds of thousands of dollars a year in his Fortune business. I see no limits to his future earning potential in this company. He has built a solid organization that is very effective. Behind Todd's leadership, his group has overcome the doubts and fears associated with any start-up business. What is Todd pushing toward? What does he see in the future that makes him willing to sacrifice time and effort today to build his business? It's the power of residual income through network marketing. Residual income is the income generated from the continued use of the products used by customers month after month. Residual income allows us to have more control of our schedules and to have more control over our lives.

Most of us are in the business of trading time for money. We report to our jobs day after day, year after year, and we are paid solely for the amount of time we spend on the job each day. In order to be paid, we must report to work each day and essentially repeat the same set of work responsibilities. By contrast, the advantage of developing a residual income stream allows us to perform a task once and to be paid repeatedly month after month, year after year, based on the success of that one day's performance.

> *"I'd prefer to have one percent of one hundred people's effort rather than one hundred percent of my effort alone."*
>
> *–J. Paul Getty*

Furthermore, in our traditional work roles, we only receive pay for the work we produce individually. The networking industry allows us to build a team of colleagues and for us to share monetarily in the success of hundreds and even thousands of people. J. Paul Getty's viewpoint is right on the money, "I'd prefer to have one percent of one hundred people's effort rather than one hundred percent of my effort alone."

I was a bit slow to grasp how powerful this concept is, but when fully comprehended, it made such perfect sense. On one hand, I could continue to beat my head against the wall financially, working three or four jobs and bringing in only the income that I could generate by myself; or, I could start my own networking business and build a profit-sharing team.

Imagine a business that earns $500 each month on a residual basis. That $500 adds up to $6,000 each year. Before we disregard that figure as being a significant amount of income or not, take a look at what it really means. That $500 a month is the equivalent of having $100,000 saved in a certificate of deposit (CD) account with a yield of 6%. Now, most of us have been employed for however long we have been employed and we have saved whatever amount we have saved. So, how many $100,000 CDs do most people have that are drawing $6,000 a year? The answer for most is none. The answer for the rest of us, is not enough! Network marketing empowers us to build the equivalent of those $100,000 CDs that pay us residual income month after month as long as company products are being used.

We want our representatives to develop a residual income stream. We want our representatives to have money made for next year and the year after that, before the next year even gets here. It makes financial sense to put yourself into an industry that will pay for years to come. Do you want to get paid for putting the door on the house, or do you want to get paid every time someone opens the door? Do you want to get paid for installing the light switch, or do you want to get paid every time someone turns the light on or off? The choice is to get paid a little bit up front, or to get paid a little bit over and over, year after year. That's what residual income is all about.

I think Todd's onto something here! He understands that it is difficult to win a championship by himself. He knows that good teamwork is the formula for winning championships and for building residual income.

Walt Disney summed it up best: "Anything is possible when hard work is combined with belief in yourself and belief in your dreams." Including, I might add, the possibility of winning a national title for you and your family.

✳　　✳　　✳

CHAPTER

9

FUNDAMENTALS WORK

WITH ALL DUE RESPECT TO WALT DISNEY, in my wildest dreams I never envisioned myself as the founder and president of a multi-million dollar company. Although we encountered our fair share of financial struggles upon opening Fortune in January of 2001, I never panicked because I knew we were fundamentally sound in the way we were structured. We definitely experienced our share of highs and lows, but I remained constant in my belief that the proper execution of sound fundamentals separates the pretenders from the contenders.

There were three principles of business that we felt most strongly about prior to opening our company. First, we were absolutely adamant that we would carry no debt whatsoever. We continue to remain a debt-free company. We simply will not operate with debt. I feel that goal should be a cornerstone of every individual's overall financial strategy. We should all strive to carry minimal debt or no debt at all.

Secondly, we vowed never to offer public shares of our company. In 1963, Mary Kay Ash was forty-three when she started a network marketing company. She knew she wanted to utilize the network marketing business model, but she wasn't certain what product she was going to sell until the eleventh hour. She finally decided that she would offer a line of cosmetics. After several years in business, she made the decision to take her company public with offerings to shareholders. A few years later she chose to buy back all company shares.

When a company goes public, the emphasis shifts to pleasing the shareholder. I watched this same business decision occur with Excel.

We vowed never to offer public shares of our company.

I observed that the "little guy" in the field, the independent business owner, lost out because the company provided the biggest chunk of the profit to its shareholders. That's just how it works when a company goes public. Mary Kay now has no shareholders, and that's a good thing. Fortune will never go public; we will maintain control in the home office, in order to allow the "little guy" to participate fully in the most lucrative pay plan in today's networking industry.

Our third business strategy was to not tie Fortune Hi-Tech Marketing to any single product, company or industry. The idea was to have a marketing company that offered a wide variety of products that represented a wide range of industries. I felt it was crucial to form a company that was in no single particular industry, providing assurance we would not be negatively impacted by an industry downturn.

As we hoped might happen, other companies quickly noticed our growth and were eager to contract with us to offer their products through our sales force of independent representatives. By September of 2001, eight months into Fortune's existence, we had added Dish Network satellite television and Cingular Wireless cell-phone service to our original lineup of four products. Our ever-expanding product and service offerings now include General Electric, AT&T, Alltel,

Sprint, T-Mobile, Verizon, Lamas Beauty, Travelocity and True Essentials, among numerous other companies and products.

This fundamental concept has proven to be a sound business model. Our initial long distance carrier service was provided by a subsidiary of WorldCom, at that time the nation's second largest long distance phone carrier. In July of 2002, WorldCom filed for bankruptcy. Thank goodness we were not a marketing company that was tied to that single company, with long distance as our sole product. We simply affiliated with other long distance carriers, continued to grow our diversified product lineup and clicked along.

I know discussing fundamentals isn't off-the-wall exciting, but these fundamental beliefs are crucial to the success of our company, and more importantly, to the success of our representatives. Fundamentals are called fundamentals in every aspect of life, and while stressing the basics in basketball or football may not be the greatest of fun, the fun part comes with the results: winning! The teams that win championships…you better believe they have mastered the fundamentals of their sport.

Each member of our Fortune corporate team has a fundamental role in the success of the company. I am so grateful to each and every employee in our office. Fortune would not be able to operate; no doubt we would not be in business, if not for the monumental efforts of the staff members in the office. I'm thankful for them. Fortune could not exist without their dedication.

When Tommy and I decided to open Fortune Hi-Tech Marketing, we realized that hiring staff was our most critical task. We made certain to surround ourselves with people who were not only experts in their field, but who were also of the same mindset and shared our vision. Our vision was to provide an opportunity for the average, ordinary person to win big financially by giving back to the industry that had been so good to us. We had to locate and to hire people who were not selfish and who did not have personal motives as their reason for coming to work with us.

Boy, did we ever succeed! Tommy does a fabulous job in his role as Chief Executive Officer, and because he takes on the role of running the office, I am able to maximize my strengths by doing what I enjoy. He is so steady. Just like "Father Time", he comes in every day and runs the office smoothly.

If I had to come in daily and coordinate office activities, it just wouldn't be good. Shoot, I'd probably come in and feel sorry that our employees were working so hard and send them home before lunch every day! My strength, I believe, is communicating with our independent representatives. It's so exciting for me to work with the folks in the field, offering motivation and sharing business-building strategies. I travel throughout the country to meet eyeball to eyeball with our representatives. If I were tied to the office each day from nine to five, I wouldn't be able to have this quality contact in the field.

Tommy and I have always been fully aware of each other's strengths, and from that vantage point we began to assemble our staff. Our first call was to Billy Stahl. Billy played a critical role in the development of Excel Telecommunications. We knew that Billy would bring experience from a company that had achieved incredible growth and he was an invaluable resource as he provided insight for setting up the office. His advice also helped us to determine the number of staff members we should initially hire, the number of computers we should purchase and so many other office-detailed decisions. Billy continues to serve as our Senior Executive Vice President of Marketing.

Our next calls were to Jon Johnson and Glenn Gatewood. Tommy, Jon and Glenn have been friends since childhood. Jon brought us extensive knowledge and expertise in the communications field. He literally has business contacts throughout the world. Jon's a character who brings a lot of personality to our staff. I don't think I've ever seen him when he wasn't juggling two or three cell phone conversations at the same time! He continues in his role as Vice President of Business Development. Glenn is our Director of Commissions. Tommy coaxed him away from his job with the Kentucky Teachers' Retirement System, where he had the responsibility of producing over 25,000 paychecks a month. We have always said that our main office objective is to distribute checks to our representatives on time, and to this day, we have

Tommy and I have always been fully aware of each other's strengths, and from that vantage point we began to assemble our staff.

met that mandate. Glenn has to work a lot of late hours, but he understands the importance of his role and he is a guy our representatives are thankful for.

We knew we needed legal expertise and I knew just the right guy. Ken Wall, a highly respected attorney from Louisville, and I had become good friends in our days as Excel representatives. I had enormous trust in Ken and his family. He worked tirelessly to sort through all the legal details of opening a business of this magnitude. Unfortunately, Ken passed away in 2004. We are forever grateful for the legal groundwork he laid for the success of our company.

Our accountant, Barry Levy, has been with us since our inception. He is a jack-of-all-trades who is as talented and loyal as the day is long. Barry helped to establish and currently leads the company's FHTM Foundation, Fortune's charitable outreach program.

I'm awfully proud of my son Jeffrey's role in the office. He worked his way through many of the Fortune departments, and now he is the Chief Operating Officer. He understands the company philosophy inside and out. Jeffrey is a details guy and a perfectionist. I rest easy knowing that he is in place to carry Fortune for years and years to come.

Fortune conducts business on a day-to-day basis with the vision to be here for our representatives for many, many years to come. We know the way our industry is viewed by some people: "Oh, those companies are here today and gone tomorrow. Oh, you know that stuff is a pyramid scheme." Although we know the many network marketing success stories over the years, and while we know that Fortune is a legitimate marketing company representing major companies such as Dish Network, General Electric, Skytel and Verizon, we don't try to convince those who don't want to be convinced. We are in the business of fundamentally doing our job to provide an opportunity for those individuals who truly want to change their lives financially.

✳　　✳　　✳

The power of winning with fundamentals and discipline was impressed upon me during my baseball-playing days at Western Kentucky University. In my sophomore year we finished our season with a record of eleven wins and thirty-one losses. I had four wins and seven losses as a starting pitcher. The head coach who recruited me was fired. As he left I shook his hand and we almost came to tears. I didn't want the coach who recruited me to leave. Guess why? I didn't know who the next coach would be and I had no way to know if he would keep my scholarship intact or not. I worried; I was uncomfortable not knowing what the future held.

Barry Schollenberger was hired as the new coach. There was a lot of anxiety, and a lot of nervousness. The first thing he did when he arrived on campus was to clean house. Before my junior year began several players had been cut. Who your daddy was, who you knew in town, or whether or not your relatives had attended Western meant nothing to Coach Schollenberger. Three-fourths of our team that year had not been on the team the previous year. It was scary, but fortunately he kept me on the team. We used to kid around and say we should be called the University of South Georgia because that's where the majority of our team was from. At least six starters, who weren't on the team the year before, were from Georgia and Florida.

We got a little better my junior year. Coach Schollenberger's message was clear: "We will be the most fundamentally sound team in the conference." We improved to a record of nineteen wins and twenty-six losses. The following year we won the Ohio Valley Conference. I was 9-4 that year as a starting pitcher, and because of a lot of outstanding play from my teammates, I was voted to the all-conference team. My gosh, I learned there was power in getting back to the "basics" of baseball.

Just think, we had finished at the bottom of the conference two years before. I had a losing record on the mound. I did not realize it at the time, but getting back to the fundamentals of baseball was absolutely the best thing that could have ever happened to us. It wasn't easy. Practices were hard and we went over and over the fundamentals of the game, but it made my college playing days worth remembering, because if my last two years had gone the way my first two years had gone, I probably would have done my best to forget my playing days. Sometimes people leaving our lives, whether it's by our choice or by their choice, seems just horrible at that moment. Sometimes, though, it is just meant to happen. Somebody who leaves our lives never controls our destiny. Don't fight it—there is always a plan.

We all know there are certain things we need to separate ourselves from in order to maximize our capabilities. Before we can be promoted in life, we must separate ourselves from what has gone on before. Once we identify those obstacles, we must discipline ourselves to focus on the appropriate path to success. Each of us must ask the question, "What do I need to separate myself from?" Hey, getting out of bed at 12:00 noon ain't gonna cut it!

So what happens even when we work hard and are disciplined, yet life doesn't seem to be working out the way we want it to or thought it would? It goes back to what I've said so many times in my life. I've always believed that something good's gonna happen if I just continue to hang on. I know something good's gonna happen, even if things don't work out the way I had planned.

Fundamentally, networking is about going out and meeting people. It's about doing the things we say we are going to do.

We don't control our habits; our habits control us. The key is to make sure our habits are good ones. I have found that it takes about ninety days for me to establish a habit. I call it the "ninety-day miracle." If I can do something for ninety days, it becomes habit. I believe when we apply healthy fundamentals for ninety days to eating, exercising, working our business, to whatever we choose, then good habits have been established.

Bob DeCant and Joanne McMahon are fundamentally building their Fortune business. They are building at the Regional, Executive and National levels. Joanne is an excellent trainer. Bob is extremely outgoing and supports the representatives on a daily basis. They are not counting on one individual to take them to the top, but are working at every level of their business to develop consistent growth. Their financial future is not in the hands of any one person or any one group.

They do a wonderful job of fundamentally training the people in their organization. They don't merely train them once and wish them the best of luck. They conduct ongoing training sessions and meet with representatives to update them on the best business building strategies. They don't just recruit and then forget about people.

Terry and Sandi Walker also do a tremendous job with the fundamentals of their business. They are especially strong with the relationship end of our business. They care about their business associates; they are good to people. Their colleagues love them and so do I.

Fundamentally, networking is about going out and meeting people. It's about doing the things we say we are going to do—if we say we are going to meet someone at Shoney's, be on time and meet them there—fundamentally treat people as you would have them treat you. I hear about shortcuts, such as primarily growing the business on the Internet, but there is no substitute for getting out there and communicating with people face to face.

Achieving success in this business is not so much about being a great speaker or possessing higher intellect. I think it's more about being able to relate to people. Even when people start to earn a significant amount of money, the ones who are able to push on even further are the ones who can still relate to those new representatives coming into their business. Those successful representatives who remember the early struggles and the questions and doubts that came with the early days of starting their own business, relate in a way to new representatives that helps them get off to a great start. In turn, this relationship building helps to explode their personal businesses. Now that doesn't mean they would want to return to that time of early struggle, but we must be able to constantly identify with the various stages that individuals in our organization are experiencing in their own businesses. This thought has always helped me to identify with every single representative who comes into our business. I remember that at some stage of my personal network marketing business, I was positioned where they are.

I don't want people to think that they have to make this gigantic leap from starting their business to becoming a millionaire overnight. There are fundamental steps to take as you are building your business. One step leads to another and you have to go through the whole process before you can reach the financial level you desire.

We must travel light in order to be successful in any business. As much as we may like to, we can't carry everybody in the world with us. We have to take the willing. In our type of business, too many times we try to convince people that they should want to do better financially for themselves and for their families. We can't do it. We can't drag people across the finish line in a headlock! We can't try and try and try to keep people fired up and excited about this financial opportunity. We don't need to call them one more time for a training session. We don't need to call them one more time to try and convince them to bring somebody to the business presentation. We don't need to call them and convince them to go to one more corporate event. It really is easier to give birth in our business than it is to raise the dead. We can't keep trying to do mouth-to-mouth. Sometimes, in business terms, we have to bury the dead. That is such a difficult concept for most of us, and it has been extremely hard for me over the years. It's tough because most of us are good, decent folks who don't ever, ever want to give up on someone whom we want to succeed in this business.

However, as a person striving to build our business, we only have a limited amount of time. We must spend that precious time with people who are willing to pay somewhat of a price to win. Sure, everybody wants to win as long as their sponsor or upline person is willing to do everything for them. Well, that's not much of a price to pay, and eventually that person will not win. We can't spend our time equally across the board. Often, we can't even spend our time where it is needed. We must spend our time where it is required. We have to spend our time where it is most beneficial to our business. That choice almost always favors the people in our organization who are working. We can't spend time with the person we like the most or who has been our buddy the longest. If we are in business to make money, then the fundamentals of our business tell us we have to spend our time where we think it is going to reward our business the most. Then, if we choose to, we can give our money away to those people we like!

Larry Bird, the great Indiana State and Boston Celtic Hall of Fame basketball legend, once said, "Master the fundamentals first." I share in that philosophy. When the team I coached at Boyle County High School won the first district championship in school history, it was because we worked every day in practice on the basic fundamentals of the game. Day after day, we worked on dribbling, shooting and passing the ball over and over again. We worked on the basic fundamentals of defending our opponent. Maybe I didn't know a whole lot about the X's and O's of basketball, and I'm sure I never drew up great plays on the chalkboard at halftime, but I believe we were successful as a team because we practiced the basic fundamentals of the game. Contenders? Pretenders? Contenders master the fundamentals because fundamentals work!

✳   ✳   ✳

10

CALLING YOUR
OWN SHOTS

LAST SPRING SHERYL AND I had a crew of workers come out to take care of some much-needed painting inside our home. During one of our conversations, I explained to them that when I was younger I was a painter. They were shocked. They didn't believe me.

"No way! You? You didn't paint houses!"

It's no big deal. We are where we are in life. That doesn't mean that is necessarily where we want to be or where we have to be and it doesn't mean that's where we are going to stay. But, yep. I know about scraping. I know about sanding. I know about climbing ladders and about fightin' wasps.

"How did you get where you are now?"

"I got tired of painting houses."

"Well, we're tired of painting houses too!"

We all do a self-evaluation from time to time and we either like where we are in life, or we understand in our own mind that there is something more we were meant to be. While I was teaching and coaching, I wasn't miserable. I enjoyed the kids, but I knew there was so much more in life that I wanted to accomplish.

Mrs. Medaris was my favorite teacher in grade school. She taught eighth grade English. Her goal as a teacher was not to get the students to think more highly of her, but to get her students to think more highly of themselves. Mrs. Medaris kept me after school one afternoon. In those days we had to write on the chalkboard a hundred times to remind us that we shouldn't have been doing whatever it was we were doing. While I was writing over and over again, "I will not stick gum underneath my chair," Mrs. Medaris commented that my handwriting was pretty. That made me feel good. No one had ever said anything about my handwriting before, good or bad. I will never forget her next words. "Paul, I'm not sure why your grades aren't all that great and you don't always pay attention in class like you should, but I really think you are going to do something huge someday. You have something special inside of you. I really believe you will do something big with your life." I was thirteen at the time, and I'm not sure if she meant it, but her praise made such an impression on me. I still smile today when I think about hearing Mrs. Medaris speak those words of encouragement.

I believe a lot of our representatives in Fortune possess the same quality of leadership that Mrs. Medaris showed me many years ago. To be successful in business, our focus must always be on the other person. Yes, we are in business to earn a living. Yes, there are times when we are starving and we've got to generate some income to feed our family. Yes, we have dreams for ourselves that we are trying to reach. Yes, yes, yes. But if we don't make it about the other person, we don't have anybody in our organization to help us build our business.

I signed Jim Voight into the Excel business in August of 1992. His wife, Kietha, called me and said that Jim had quit his teaching and coaching job to work this Excel business and she was scared to death.

She explained, "We don't have much money and Jim is so focused on this one thing. Paul, can you really make a living in this business?" Well, I was still scared to death myself, but I knew it could be done.

I hopped in my truck and immediately drove to their home in Illinois to visit them. I sat down on their couch and made a commitment to them that day. "Here is what I promise you. I will work with you to the best of my ability, and I will come and see you as many times as I need to come and see you to help you get this business off to a great start. I will be here as much as you want me to be here."

She said, "Okay, that's good enough for me."

A lot of times that's all people want to know, that we will be there for them when and if help is really needed. Occasionally, they just want to pick up the phone and hear a reassuring voice on the other end of the line. We have to step up as leaders. We can't say, "Sure, you can do it—now, you go out there and get 'em." We won't get any results from that approach. We have to say, "Yes, it can be done. Let's go get 'em together." People have to know how much you care, before they care how much you know.

Genuinely caring about the people in our organization is where the wisdom of leadership begins. When we genuinely care about someone, we are willing to sacrifice our time and efforts to help them achieve success. We will know when that person needs to hear words of encouragement. We will know when they need to be motivated in a nice way. We will know when they need to be loved on in a nice way. John Quincy Adams said, "If your actions inspire others to dream more, learn more, do more and become more, you are a leader." There are times we need to let those around us hear that we don't know everything, and times they need to hear that they don't either. Even though we are in there fighting for ourselves, fighting to make our business grow, it cannot be done without the help of others. If we take care of the other person and help them earn some money, the "us" part of our business will be taken care of.

All of us have different strengths and weaknesses that surface as we build our business and help those in our organization build their businesses. That's perfectly normal, just as we realize different vehicles are made for various purposes. If we want to travel in the snow, there is a particular vehicle that will help with our traction. If we are hauling a boat somewhere, we need a certain vehicle to carry heavy loads. If we are traveling long distances, we want a vehicle that will allow us to maintain good gas mileage.

This same philosophy applies to our Fortune business. We can't make all people fit all roles for all occasions; it's just not possible. It's kind of like a track relay team. The coach takes advantage of each runner's strengths by placing him or her in the position where they can help the team perform its best. One runner may start quickly, another runner may be the best through that "middle mile," and yet another runner may be the strong "closer" in the race. The entire team wins when each runner is allowed to perform to his or her strengths. In other words, some representatives are more comfortable speaking in front of large groups. Others prefer face-to-face meetings with no more than a few present. As leaders we can help identify the areas where individuals in our organization are strong and work together to build a much more effective team.

Disagreements are inevitable. It's not possible to be on the same page all the time with our friends, our family or our business associates. As we grow to care about individuals, we must remember our own imperfections. There are times we will offend others, even though we certainly do not intend to. Other times we will be offended or hurt by someone close to us. In almost all cases there is a time to forgive, to forget and to move on.

Ulysses S. Grant made a powerful comment at the end of the Civil War. When Robert E. Lee surrendered to Grant at Appomattox Courthouse in 1865, some of the Northern generals wanted to punish General Lee and the Confederate soldiers. There was talk of beatings and of hangings. Grant was asked by one of his commanders, "What will we do with them now, sir?"

Grant's response was that there had been enough suffering, "Forget it. The war is over." There are times in our leadership when we should take General Grant's advice and just "forget it" and move forward. There are times when someone did this or didn't do that; or we thought they should have said this, or were going to say that. Hey, all of us fall short of being perfect.

"It's easy for 'those people.' They were born to lead."

I always hear that. I don't believe it for a second. We all have different traits within us that we bring forth at certain times in our lives and many of us have talents within us that never surface. In fact, most of the time, our special qualities only come out when they are forced out of us.

*   *   *

In the Bible, David was good at one thing: slinging rocks! Even though he was only sixteen years old, he had shepherded his father's flock for several years. He became an expert marksman with his slingshot because of this experience, a trait that was necessary to protect his flock from wolves and other predatory animals. One day his father, Jesse, sent him to the front line of Saul's army to take food and supplies to his older brothers. As soon as he arrived, he heard talk of the great Philistine warrior, Goliath. Every morning, Goliath would come to the top of the hill and shout out the same challenge to Saul's army.

If anyone would meet him in an individual battle, the winner would be the victor of the entire war between the Philistines and Israelites. David stepped forward to fight the Philistine.

David equated this challenge, of defending his people in a showdown against Goliath, with protecting his family's flock of sheep. David chose five smooth stones out of a nearby brook and put them in his shepherd pouch. He met Goliath on the battlefield, carrying his staff, his five stones, and most of all, his faith in the Lord. David whirled his handpicked stone through the air, struck Goliath in the forehead and killed him.

We can't change who we are or try to become something we're not in our effort to chase success...We are who we are and we don't need to copy anyone else.

David's fame spread to every corner of the kingdom. His triumph over Goliath gave him the opportunity to gain the confidence of the people of Israel. David led many armies from that point and conquered much land in the name of the Lord. In life, being good at one thing can lead to other things we were meant to do with our lives. King David would never have become King David if he had not been good at slinging rocks.

I've said it a million times, "We can't disregard where we are in life." Our experience in one area might lead itself to greatness in another area of life. Our success in one area might lead to success in another area of life. We may have qualities of greatness inside of us just waiting for the opportunity to be forced out. We become successful leaders when we combine our past experiences and accomplishments with the dreams and the passion we hold for the future.

Is it important to emulate the success of others? Of course it is. We want to learn from successful people in all walks of life, and especially from those who are doing well in our business. But we can't change who we are or try to become something we're not in our effort to chase success. It just doesn't work like that. We are who we are and we don't need to copy anyone else. We will find that success comes when we combine who we are with the mixture of knowledge and experience we gain in the field on a daily basis.

I previously mentioned Ruel Morton, who is a true leader in the networking industry. He earned over one million dollars in his first full year in the Fortune business and earned over one million dollars again in his second year with our company. No one person that I know of, in any network marketing company, has ever earned more money in the first two years of his business than Ruel Morton with Fortune Hi-Tech Marketing.

Think about this. Mary Kay Cosmetics, in its forty-third year of business, had their first representative to earn one million dollars in a single year. Mary Kay is a wonderfully run company with many outstanding representatives in their organization. We have learned so much about the networking industry by observing the way Mary Kay conducts business. To realize that Ruel attained this level of financial success in his first two years, is absolutely incredible.

It has been said in many magazine articles and other publications that I made more money than any other network marketer in the shortest period of time. It is true that for several months my paycheck was over one million dollars. That financial freedom came together after six years of struggles and a lot of hard work. But remember, when I was into the second year of my business, I was looking for a way out! I could not even imagine producing that kind of income at that stage of my Excel business.

What is it that allows this kind of record-breaking financial success in two years time? Is it Ruel Morton? Is it the Fortune company?

Fortune had been in existence for four years before Ruel came to the corporate office in November of 2004. He was an Excel representative when it shut down and was offered money and various perks to join other companies. When he came to Lexington to talk about our business, I took him and a group of others to dinner at Ramsey's, a down-home, country-cooking, Kentucky restaurant. I offered him my word that I was going to do everything I could to build Fortune into the best network marketing company in the world. I also assured him that Fortune would be around for the long haul. Ruel later met with Tommy and Jon Johnson, and he talked with Billy Stahl. I have heard Ruel say that he chose to join Fortune because of its people. For sure, people do business with people. People don't do business with companies.

Ruel and his wife, Angel, live in east Texas and are such good, humble folks. They complement each other so well. Ruel knows how to motivate and peak the interest of people as they evaluate the business. Angel is the nurturer and encourages others. Once in the business, she takes care of the organization. When people get down and out, Angel gives that shoulder to cry on and helps resolve the difficult struggles that we know everyone encounters in building their own business.

Angel builds the personal relationships with the representatives in their organization that really makes their business special. She organizes visits to the ranch where they live. There, the families spend time together and visit with other families while a spouse is out working the business. They create such a warm environment in their home, where people can come for business advice as well as emotional and spiritual support.

I have traveled with Ruel and I've heard him speak. He brings home such a powerful message. We are all familiar with the Bible's message, "We reap what we sow." Ruel likes to say that we, as individuals, go to the fields each day, and we plant and water, hoe and weed, and harvest and store in the barn for somebody else. We are simply laborers who want our paycheck on Friday. We stay broke in this country because we spend our time sowing in someone else's field. We don't reap any real rewards because we are not harvesting anything for ourselves.

For sure, people do business with people. People don't do business with companies.

The owner of that field understands that by managing and overseeing his own field, the larger payday will come when the crops are sold at some particular point in the future. We need to own and work in our own fields! We need to be paid when we harvest and sell our own crop. We have a history of individuals who forged their way into prosperity through hard work and by a vision of a better tomorrow for themselves and for their family. We need to rekindle that entrepreneurial spirit that built this country. Networking provides us the vehicle to call our own shots!

What I see from Ruel and Angel is, by setting the example, they have built their business while showing others how to build their own businesses. They treat the members in their organization with respect and understanding. As a leader it is necessary to go out and show those in your organization that you are willing to pay the price to be successful in this business. Just like in other phases of life, people will do what they see us do—not what we say we are going to do. If they see that we are not supporting our representatives, that we are not gathering new customers or we are not trying to bring new people into the business, then they won't do it either. If we are showing up late to meetings and we are the first person out of the meeting when it's over, that shows the importance we place on our business to the people in our organization. And believe me, it's that way in all phases of our lives. Our children watch us and they see how we talk to Mom or talk to Dad. They see how we conduct ourselves around other people and hear what we say when others are not present.

The really neat thing about the network marketing business is that someone like Ruel is out there giving his time and effort to someone taking a look at the business. I know of no other industry where the leaders of the company take the time to talk, to interact and to answer questions for those who are not even in the business yet!

In other industries, where do we find people making huge salaries that talk to people like us? What CEO of a major corporation or leading wage earner of a company will sit down and offer us financial advice or show us a way to earn the kind of money they are making? They don't know us to take the time. They don't have the time to spend with us even if they did know us. We don't know where they reside to go find them and ask for their time. They live in a separate world!

In network marketing we get training and a how-to-guide from the leaders and the people who are out there earning large amounts of money each month. The leaders in network marketing, and in our Fortune company in particular, are focused on helping someone accomplish more in their lives than they would otherwise attempt. We want people in today's world to visualize the potential within them, and to discover a way to unleash that potential—not just financially, not in any one phase of their lives, but fundamentally, in every aspect we can live a richer life.

I acted like I had all these choices to fall back on prior to making the decision to join Excel as a representative. In reality, I had nowhere to go financially. My future, looking me square in the face, consisted of painting houses in the summer, raising tobacco and teaching school. That was my future for at least twenty-seven years, and even longer if I wanted any kind of decent retirement package. It seemed like I was looking right down the barrel of a gun. It was misery, not because of the teaching, because there are many rewards in that profession. For sure, though, it was financial misery.

The questions are, "Can I do better? Can I do better in a financial way? Can I do better in other areas of my life?" God won't ever compare me to anyone else; I will be judged against what I had the ability to achieve.

Network marketing is the little guy's chance to do something. There's nowhere else in the world that anyone has the opportunity, with such little financial risk, to do a little better, a lot better or a heck of a lot better! We all want to own more of our own time. We all want to call our own shots. I've said plenty of times, "If you are not playing a big part in your own game plan, then chances are you are part of someone else's game plan." I echo Ruel's philosophy: We need to own and work in our own fields!

✳ ✳ ✳

CHAPTER

11

It's Scripture

About six months ago i stopped at a Shoney's Restaurant in Asheville, North Carolina. It looked to me like there was a network marketing meeting in the side dining room. I knew this because I had done quite a few of those meetings myself in Shoney's all across the country. Generally, if members in your group will eat there, Shoney's will provide a side room to conduct your meeting. I asked one of the waitresses about the nature of the meeting. She told me it was a networking company called Xango. I decided to walk into the meeting and sit down. It wasn't too long until someone recognized me and said, "Hey, you're Paul Orberson. What are you doing here?"

I told them I was there to support the industry that has been so good to me. I added that I admire anybody out there working and making the effort to change the financial future for their families— "God bless every one of you." I never talked about Fortune, never even mentioned Fortune. I just really enjoyed sitting back and hearing about that company's program, while experiencing a presentation from a different point of view. It was like ballplayers talking to other ballplayers. We were able to identify with each other's victories, defeats and the struggles each of us faced.

I paid for their meals and came away feeling blessed. I really did! They seemed to be a little surprised that a president of a competing company would take the time to talk and share stories with them. It was a great experience for me to witness troops out in the field. It didn't matter to me in the least that they were some other company's troops. It was simply nice to share the evening with good folks who also happened to have a common business bond. I received the nicest thank you notes from a few of the people in attendance. I will always remember that night and cherish those notes.

We all need to give and to get from other people. It's by helping and by giving to others that we actually strike that chord within us that helps us feel good about ourselves, that helps us believe in a better tomorrow. We need to treat people right, regardless of whether they can or ever will be able to help us in our business. We need to treat people right, whether they will ever be able to help us in our personal lives. It's Scripture and the giver's soul is touched more than the receiver's.

Growing up, every time the church doors opened we were there. Sunday morning, Sunday night, Wednesday night, we were in church for every service. We were involved in every activity the church had to offer—Vacation Bible School, softball, RA's. I have early memories of being told if we were good during Sunday morning services, we could go out to eat afterwards. It was very rare for us to go out, so we behaved well most of the time. We would go to the Rosemont Grill on Harrodsburg Road, just a mile from where the current Fortune office is located. The first prayer I learned was, "God is great. God is good. Now I thank Him for our food." Mike, Karen and I would take turns before every meal reciting that prayer.

My mother and father gave me my first Bible when I was eight years old. The Bible is the single biggest influence in my life today. I am thankful to God for everything I have in my life. It is true— "Every good gift and every perfect gift cometh down from the Father above."

I know it is a common perception that most wealthy people are wasteful, spoiled, arrogant and selfish, among other unflattering adjectives. In my opinion, having a lot of money does not change a person; having a lot of money just makes us more of what we are. Or, it makes us more of what we are not. Money doesn't make a person arrogant, spoiled, wasteful or selfish. There are plenty of those people in many walks of life who don't have a bit of money. I truly believe that a person with money can do more good than a person without money.

The Bible shares the message that the Lord God gives us the power and the desire to get wealth. What we do with wealth is merely an extension of who we are as a person in this life. Whether we have a lot or whether we have a little, I encourage us all to be givers. We are blessed to be a blessing to others. By all means our command to give is certainly not just about money. Heck, we know that each and every one of us has time to give. We have a helping hand to give. We can give and share our knowledge. We have kind words to give. We have a shoulder to give. I have no doubt in my mind that the givers of this world sleep better at night, have a more positive outlook on the day ahead, are more healthy, and live a fuller life than those who are not givers.

The very same principle applies to our Fortune business. Fortune was not started for any personal profit motive. It most definitely was not. The reason for the launch of the company was to give back, and to give those individuals willing to work an opportunity to build financial security in their lives. As a company, we pay for cars for our representatives, we pay for hotel rooms, we pay for airline tickets, and we give raises all the time. Honest to goodness, our profit margin continues to grow month after month. From a business standpoint, the company is so strong simply because of the fundamental business structure we have in place. The more we give, the bigger and stronger Fortune becomes.

Beyond all of that thankful-ness, though, we've still got to get off our rear ends and do our share of the workload!

Scripture tells us that if we are mindful, it is God in our life who blesses us, and that He will further bless us with more health, more wealth, and fuller relationships. Those words have definitely proven true in my life. As I have learned, though, God does not work alone in our lives. We have to be willing to do our share of the work.

I like the story of the farmer who bought an old farm on the out-skirts of town. Grass and weeds were growing over most of the farm, and the house on the property was a wreck. It had been in shambles for years and years. The farmer moved in and worked and worked for three years on his new place. He mowed the fields, repaired the fences, hanged and secured all the gates, ploughed and planted a garden, re-paired and painted the house. Then one day a visitor walked up to the place and said, "Man, oh man! Look what God has given you. He has blessed you with this wonderful, beautiful farm."

The farmer looked around over the grounds, admired the new look of his farm, then responded to the visitor, "You should have seen this place when God had it all by himself!"

Yes, God blesses us. Yes, I'm thankful for all He has done in my life. Yes, I would be nothing without His grace and love for me. Be-yond all of that thankfulness, though, we've still got to get off our rear ends and do our share of the workload!

That is why I am so proud of someone like Jerry Brown. He grew up in the Bronx, New York, and is a twenty-year retired military man. He served our country in the first Gulf War, then returned home to pastor his church in Atlanta, Georgia. In two-and-a-half years after joining Fortune, Jerry worked his way to total financial independence. It absolutely thrills me to send great big checks to Jerry month after month. He has absolutely earned every bit of the money he makes through his hard work and persistence to achieve. Jerry has helped countless numbers of folks through his personal efforts to make a difference in the lives of others.

Jerry has a heart bigger than a racehorse. His focus is helping others to succeed. I notice when I'm around him the way that he loves people. He and his wife, Deborah, and daughter, April, are such quality people. They are the kind of people with whom you would want to build your business. Jerry has primarily worked in the pastoral community, because that is where he sees the need for our business. He has seen how the additional funds generated by his Fortune business have allowed him to give and to provide in areas that he never could before. His business continues to grow, as does his heart, right along with the success of his relationships.

Jerry Brown was willing to start his Fortune business before he knew how it was going to turn out. He showed faith in the company and a strong belief in the people that introduced him to Fortune. He is now financially independent making hundreds of thousands of dollars a year, and those numbers are on the rise. It's rewarding for me to see that a good family man, with no particular advanced training, is able to show that with desire and effort anything is possible.

✳   ✳   ✳

I realize the importance of our company in the lives of our Fortune Representatives. For many, this is their opportunity to compete for the national title for their family. It is a big deal for the financial future of many, many people. On the other hand, we must keep every aspect of our life in perspective. I try to convey this message to our representatives, that although our financial standing is an important part of what we are able to do with our lives, it is still just one part of our lives.

Fortune is one aspect of our representatives' lives. Fortune is one part of my life, of Tommy's and of Jeff's life. The other staff members at the home office give so much to our Fortune company, yet it is still just one part of all of their lives. Many of us have children and some of us have grandchildren. We have friends outside of the business. We have church functions to which we devote a lot of time and effort. There are people in the business world that think it's an all or nothing commitment to be financially successful in life. I don't buy that. I actually think that anyone who focuses all their efforts on the financial part of life and neglects the other areas necessary for a well-balanced life will become the most depressed person in the world. There are more parts to our lives than just the monetary aspect. We shouldn't sacrifice everything. It's important to stop and smell the roses along the way.

We must strive to develop every aspect of who we are, explore inside, expand our knowledge, our relationships and our interests in other areas of life. We can balance our lives by giving time to our personal well-being, as well as to our financial well-being. I want Fortune representatives to have a life outside of the business. We want our representatives to enjoy the fruits of their labor.

Heck, Ruel and Angel couldn't stop the growth of their business even if they wanted, but Ruel struggled before he found financial success through network marketing. Angel was a single mom before she met Ruel. I believe one of the reasons for their great success is that they do remember where they came from. They received help from individuals when they were in need of help. Now, Ruel and Angel are the ones able to reach out as that light of hope to others in need.

Now that the financial part of their lives is on track, they have the opportunity to reap the rewards of these efforts over the past few years. They can focus on areas of interest to them. It just so happens that like so many of our representatives, Ruel and Angel like to spend their time, energy and money giving back.

Ruel and Angel give to their church. I know they give to their parents and take care of so many others. I'm sure they would never tell this story themselves, but I think it is important to know how much good can be done by those who have the hearts to give.

Last Christmas, Ruel and Angel chose forty-five underprivileged children and spent three weeks buying items from their Santa Claus wish list. I know that was so satisfying for them to be able to put a smile on their faces. They also bought Christmas dinners for the children's families and involved the whole church in delivering and making a special holiday gift a reality for them. Wow! This was not about the money for Ruel and Angel. This was just two good folks doing something out of the kindness of their hearts for these young people and their families. As much joy as I'm sure that brought to those families, I still believe that the giver in every case is blessed way beyond our imagination.

Solomon advises, "In all your getting, get understanding." What's so hard to understand about the power of giving? We are charged by Scripture not only to give, but also to provide an inheritance for our children, as well as for our children's children. Indeed, to leave financial help for our family is the right thing to do. But it's not so much the monetary value of "stuff" left behind; it's the heart-felt devotion to those we love, so they may understand that we care enough about them to assure financial stability into their future.

Family, as we all know, can be one of our greatest sources of happiness. Family is also the very thing that can lead to much heartache. We share our private moments with those who are closest to us. Brothers, sisters, spouses, parents and other family members have been there during our ups and downs. They praise us and they disagree with us. Loved ones are our best friends at times and at other times can become very distant. We can share our dreams with them; yet, when they don't agree with the choices we make, it can be very hurtful. It always seems those family fences can be the hardest ones to mend. The giving of ourselves is so difficult at times. But, when we are able to forgive and forget our past disagreements, we benefit by the cleansing of our own soul. It's never too late to start anew.

Consider the Bible story of Joseph's big dream. He had a vision that he would grow up to be a person of great importance. He shared his dream with his family. Each and every family member basically laughed in his face. Some family members asked Joseph who he thought he was to have such a dream. Eventually, his family became angry with him. In fact, his brothers became so angered with him that they sold him into slavery. Although Joseph became a slave, he kept his belief strong and his faith in the Lord never wavered. Joseph maintained the outlook that something good was going to happen in his life. He was right. He was promoted out of slavery into a position in the household of Potiphar, a high-ranking executive in the Egyptian government. Potiphar observed Joseph and believed that he was a good, honest person. He placed Joseph in charge of his entire estate holdings.

Shortly thereafter Potiphar's wife tried to seduce Joseph. When Joseph refused her attempts, she accused him of making advances on her. Once again Joseph was demoted into slavery. He knew he hadn't done anything wrong. Ultimately, Joseph again proved himself to be trustworthy and he continued to believe that through God, something good was gonna happen. Sure enough, Joseph was promoted time and again until he became second in command of all of Egypt. Through his faith, courage and determination not to abandon his childhood dream, Joseph did become a person of great importance.

It's not so much the monetary value of "stuff" left behind; it's the heart-felt devotion to those we love, so they may understand that we care enough about them to assure financial stability into their future.

Years passed and a famine struck other parts of the world; starving citizens came from miles around to beg for food. Incredibly, right before Joseph's eyes came the very brothers who had ridiculed him and sold him into slavery. Joseph found himself positioned to help his family in need. He chose to forgive their transgressions and to give them the food and help they needed. Joseph brought his entire family to Egypt and gave them the best lands in the country.

Giving is the living proof that the cancer of greed hasn't eaten our souls. It may sound strange, but it's true that the more we give the more we receive. I know, as I have witnessed over the years, that money may leave our hands, but it never leaves our lives. Every time I have given in my life, it has stayed in my life and has come back to bless me in uncountable measure. It's Scripture.

If I can encourage anything at all in this book it would be for us all to give as we go. For me, people think when I give I'm giving to the other person and to a certain extent I am. But I give without expecting anything in return. I don't care if anyone else knows what I give or how much I give. I know! The people and organizations I give to also know. I give for me because it's good for my soul.

I feel so fortunate to be around and to witness so many true givers in our business. I believe there is so much more going on than just the accumulation of a lot of money. There is a giving nature among our representatives that has touched more lives than we will ever know. How much should we give? When we decide that we want to help and we want to give, we will know what we can give and who needs the help.

We view Betty Miles as a great success story in the networking industry, but she had to overcome the doubts of close family members to be able to give hope to so many in her home state. Her husband, Jim, was Secretary of State for South Carolina. Betty made the decision to sign up with Excel in the early 1990's. Of course, Jim's job was to regulate every type of business coming and going within the state borders. At first, he was very upset at the thought of Betty being involved with a network marketing company. He warned her of pyramid schemes and encouraged her not to get involved with one of "those companies," because they are "here today and gone tomorrow."

She explained to her husband that the networking industry had changed over the last twenty years, and there were laws in every state to regulate these types of companies. She pleaded with her husband to research the legitimacy of the industry. Betty knew the one thing she could count on from her husband was that he was fair. So he examined the Excel business and found it to be legitimate. As Betty proved the earning power of the networking industry, Jim came around to believe in its wealth-building power as well. He also came to appreciate the industry for bringing much needed business income into the state of South Carolina.

Betty and Jim chose to invest the majority of the money they made from Excel. In turn, they used the dollars earned on these investments to impact their state and community in positive ways. They built a six-thousand square foot home in the mountains, complete with eight bedrooms and training rooms, which they allow their church to use for retreats. It's a way of giving back. Betty helps to fund a home for battered women and children. She is also working on a project to help unwed mothers retain their children, when financially there would be no other option but to put them up for adoption. Furthermore, she is working to provide a setting where the mothers will be able to work while their babies are being provided with childcare. Betty is also pushing to build a network of Fortune Representatives who can alternate childcare with working the Fortune business.

What a great purpose! What a great feeling Betty must have going to bed at night knowing she is helping and giving in a big way!

I have always believed the best thing you can do for the less fortunate is not to be one of them. If we can earn enough to provide for ourselves and for our family, that's good. If we can earn enough to take care of all our needs and then be able to help someone else, that's giving back. That's living the good life.

I've read before that money is like manure. If you pile it up, it stinks. But if you spread it around, it does a lot of good. We are to be a river with our money, not a pond or a dammed up body of water. Our money is to be like a flowing body of water to help improve the lives of others.

* * *

CHAPTER

12

ONE HUNDRED TIMES BETTER!

IN 1995, I PURCHASED A NEW CHEVY TAHOE at a Tampa car
dealership. I wrote a check for $27,800 and drove it off the lot. It was
the first vehicle I had fully paid for in my life. I had leased cars and
made payments, but this was the first time I had actually bought, paid
for and completely owned my own "ride." It was really nice, a pretty
red color that shined in the Florida sunlight with all the works; it had
tinted windows, leather seats and a cassette player.

I had an overwhelmingly proud feeling inside! That Tahoe was significant confirmation in my mind that I was winning in my financial
life. "Look Orberson," I thought, "you won't be borrowing any more
money for cars in your lifetime." Heck, I knew I wouldn't need to bor-
row money for anything ever again. What a great feeling that was!

I thought about financial success and what that meant to me. My
checks were hundreds of thousands of dollars each month and I knew
what was coming in the next month and the month after that—hundreds of thousands of dollars. My financial success signaled to me that
I had overcome the struggles of the past couple of years and that I had
made it to the place I wanted to be—financial independence.

As I drove around in my Tahoe, I felt like a kid again! I remember thinking about some of the things that, as a kid, gave me a good feeling inside. I thought about all the times I came in after playing a ballgame and Mom had my favorite meal on the table: hamburgers and fries. The fries always had a lot of salt on them. Yum, yum! That was so good! I remember once or twice a year my father took us to see my favorite team, the Cincinnati Reds, play baseball in old Crosley Field. I loved listening to the Reds play on the radio, but that was no comparison to seeing them play in person. The stadium looked so big! It was just like a dream come true to actually see Tony Perez, Johnny Bench, Jim Maloney and all the Reds in person playing the game I loved so much.

As kids we dream big! We dream of living in castles, of being kings and queens, of reaching higher, going further and of accomplishing whatever our imaginations tell us we can accomplish.

As I continued to think about those childhood memories, it hit me! While growing up, Mom and Dad shouldered all the financial worries for our family. Whatever I needed, I knew they would provide. As a kid my mind was free to dream and I spent many days thinking about all the spectacular things I would do, the places I would see and the lifestyle I would enjoy.

When we are kids, we place no limits on the possibilities that are ahead of us. We are inspired by everything this life has to offer. We don't dream of going to work in a Ford motor plant, not that there is anything wrong with a Ford motor plant, but my point is that it's not what we dream about. As kids we dream big! We dream of living in castles, of being kings and queens, of reaching higher, going further and of accomplishing whatever our imaginations tell us we can accomplish. Cruising in my Tahoe, I had those same feelings once again. I had no financial worries and my mind was free to dream again.

Before I started in Excel I had almost given up on my dreams. I was thirty-three years old and felt like I was in a very common situation. I had two kids and had worked my job as a teacher and a coach for thirteen years. I was in the routine of going to work for someone else each day and was picking up enough of a paycheck each month to barely stay broke. I had tried to work a few jobs on the side, but it seemed like I was always working yet never earning enough money to stay ahead of the game.

I was at the point that I started thinking, "Hey, maybe if I help Jeffrey and Sarah to be all they can be then that will help me feel good about where I am in my life." We sometimes do this as parents. As our own dreams begin to fade, we start to dream big for our kids. We work and try to set things up for them to have it better than we did. We want our children to have more and be able to do more than us. We send them to the best camps or buy them the best shoes or get them the latest, greatest thing out there. We do everything in our power to help our children live out their dreams.

We say to our kids, "Follow your dreams! Don't let anybody tell you that you can't do something you want to do with your life. You can grow up to be anything you want to be." We deliver this message, yet we aren't out there pushing to become everything we want to be. We aren't out there chasing our dreams. I realize that my most precious gifts on this earth are Jeffrey and Sarah. I thank God every day for the blessing of having children in my life. However, being Sarah and Jeffrey's daddy can't be my only purpose in life. They have lives of their own and I have a life of my own. I know I'm responsible for setting the example for Jeffrey and Sarah. Through me I want them to see the lifetime benefits of pursuing their own dreams.

I experienced some real scary times early in Excel. There were times when I didn't know what was going to be on my next paycheck—times I wasn't sure there was going to be anything at all on my next paycheck. I had to work my way into the feeling of winning. I took one step at a time. There were setbacks along the way, but I pressed on, knowing I could either make excuses or make money, but I couldn't do both.

Also, I knew I wanted to be in charge of more of my own time. I wanted to make decisions based on what I wanted for my family, not on my financial limitations. I didn't want someone telling me what time my lunch hour would be. I didn't want someone else telling me when my family could go on vacation. I was ready, willing and able to chase my dream of financial independence.

What's wrong with dreaming again at age thirty-three? What's wrong with dreaming again at age forty-three, fifty-three or whatever age we may be? Why can't we rekindle some of those childhood dreams that kept us smiling and gave us a bounce in our step as kids? Those dreams made us look forward to the next day and to the future, with excitement about all the possibilities ahead for us. Why can't we be out there setting the example for our children? Pursuing our dreams is what makes life, life!

Dreams change as we get older and I understand that. By the time I began marketing the long distance phone service for Excel, I no longer dreamed of playing major league baseball. I no longer dreamed of becoming a lawyer. I had worked the tobacco crops, painted houses and gotten into rental property with Tommy to try and better my family's financial future. Now, I dreamed of being financially independent and calling my own shots.

Chasing dreams ain't easy. Many times we find that it is not popular with our friends and family to step out of where we are in our lives. In many cases we are trying to live out our dreams, which points out to others how far they are from living out their dreams. This can happen without us saying a word. When we step out and try to improve ourselves in the financial world, we aren't condemning anyone. Many times it is more comfortable for the ones around us if we merely "maintain our place" in life, because they want to avoid the thought of removing themselves from their comfort zone.

Is it hard to row against the tide? Is it difficult when we don't receive the support of some of our friends and family? Absolutely. Was it worth it for me? You betcha! Those times of doubt, the times of struggle, the times of questioning myself, are exactly the times I reflect on now to help me realize the good times are so extraordinarily good.

I think back on some of the most important lessons I've learned in my life and I realize I'm still a work in progress. My financial independence has allowed me to focus on so many other meaningful areas of my life. I have learned that we have to take care of our bodies if we want to live a productive, healthy life. We have to eat right and exercise regularly.

We must also exercise spiritually! I read my Bible every day and I am constantly praying for everyone and everything in my life to be of honor to God. One of the most important lessons I have learned is to give and to serve others. We need to give and to serve in all areas of our lives. Martin Luther King, Jr. stated it best: "Everyone can be great because anybody can serve. You don't have to have a college degree to serve. You don't have to make your subject and your verb agree to serve. You only need a heart full of grace, a soul generated by love." I have witnessed and I certainly believe that those who give in the service of others always benefit the most.

The fruits of sacrifice really hit me the first fifteen to twenty minutes each morning after I wake up. I realize then that my whole day is going to be so different in a good way because of what went on years ago during my times of struggle. Sometimes I think back to those winters in college when we lived in the trailer. I remember the year our hot water heater went out and how we heated pans of water on the stove so we could take a lukewarm bath at night. Then I immediately fast forward. It feels really good to know when the cold weather hits Kentucky, if our water heater goes out, I feel confident that I can afford to replace it! I'm proud that each day I get to wake up and say, "Good morning, Lord," instead of thinking, "Good Lord, it's morning." Winning in my financial life has been one hundred times better than I ever dreamed.

It's not as though I think I have arrived. I've never felt that way. I'm always striving to do better in every aspect of my life and that's healthy for me. It is always a matter of where we focus our energy. What will our priorities be for today? What will we strive to accomplish tomorrow?

✳   ✳   ✳

While I was gaining my financial independence, I enjoyed so many great moments along the way. When my Excel business began to take off I opened an office in Danville. My mother managed the office. She handled all the calls and scheduled my meetings. I really enjoyed that. She was so wonderful. I remember a special time when she went to the Excel National Convention with me and got to meet a lot of the representatives she had spoken with on the phone. She couldn't believe it! She was actually a celebrity. Everyone hugged her and told her how much they appreciated her. She realized she was helping a lot of people and it made me feel so good to see her taking it all in and feeling good about what she was doing for others.

I remember calling Jeffrey while he was in college and saying, "Hey, let's go somewhere this week." We went to Hawaii! It was his first trip there. We had a great time. We went to the golf course where the PGA plays the Mercedes-Benz Championship and we visited the many coral reef spots on the islands. Mostly, we hung out together, ate and walked the beaches. It was so relaxing. What a great opportunity to spend quality time with my son!

I am such a conservative person by nature that I am often kidded about not taking extravagant vacations or buying luxury items for myself. So when I do buy a little something for myself, it is a big deal. Even though I have either lived by the ocean or had a home near the ocean for many years, I just purchased my first boat. Tommy, Jeff, Jon and I recently traveled to my South

My mother couldn't believe it! She was actually a celebrity. Everyone hugged her and told her how much they appreciated her.

Carolina home for a business retreat. We wanted to get away to brainstorm and kick around some ideas for advancing Fortune. We figured the fresh ocean air would help relax us and clear our minds, so we decided to test out the boat. We went to the Charleston Harbor, untied it from the boat dock and cruised around. I've never boated much, but it felt great to be at the wheel. I think I was making the guys a little nervous as I weaved the boat in and out and past the USS Yorktown. It is a huge ship, but we just kept puttering along taking in the fresh air and the view of all the ships in the harbor. Then Jeff asked, "What is that island in the distance?" It was Fort Sumter, the location of the first shots of the Civil War. We decided to go check it out.

It took awhile for us to make it all the way out to the fort. Once there we were able to get really close. We could see the lower and the upper levels where the cannons protected the fort. I had so much fun! We laughed and cut up and really had a relaxing time. Those are moments I cherish. Those are the times I feel like all the work and all the effort have paid off for me in such a big way.

I get that same good feeling every time I have an opportunity to see Sarah ride her horses. I see the enjoyment in her eyes every time she mounts up. I remember buying her first horse when she was seven years old. We started out with a little pony named March. Sarah loved that horse and kept it for almost ten years. Over the years she's had several horses and continues to travel and ride in competitions across the country. Riding is her passion. Sarah goes to the stable every day. I can't even imagine her life without the fulfillment she receives from her horses.

I admit that it makes me proud to be able to provide my children with opportunities they may never have experienced. I want to leave behind more than just a monetary inheritance; I want to leave behind memories and times together. I want to set an example of a healthy lifestyle and of spiritual awareness. I want to strive to form good habits, and set good examples in all areas of my life. Not only do I want to leave more than money to my children, I also want to leave something for my children's children.

Jeff and his wife, Ashley, have two children, William Jeffrey and Carter Elizabeth. It feels wonderful to help them build for their financial futures. Jeff and I both contribute to their savings each month. However, the best feeling is to be here to see them grow, to learn and to enjoy life. Right now I can hold them, play with them and spend time with them. Because of the difficult times I have been through, I am able to appreciate the special moments with all of my family. I have not and will not take life for granted. Every single time I see my kids or my grandchildren I recognize that it could be the last time. It's not a negative way of living life; it's just the realization that I need to cherish every moment of every day. I look at Will and Carter and I know that someday they will attend the college of their choice. They have the opportunity to dream big.

I'm happy that Fortune is a place where Jeff can always work and help people. Sarah, if she decides to do so, will always have a place to work. My dream at this stage of my life is for Fortune to continue way beyond Tommy and me. I envision Fortune retreats occurring ten, fifteen, twenty years from now, where there are discussions of longevity regarding the company and of ways to make it even stronger.

We want Fortune to be here for the children of our representatives. We have so many Fortune Representatives making a full-time income in our business. We realize every decision we make has a huge impact on a lot of people in our company and accept that as a serious responsibility. We know there are representatives who have reached financial independence and many more who are on their way.

For instance, I know Joel McNinch is well on his way to winning in his financial life. He's working to get the whole state of Michigan and beyond on fire with "Fortune fever." Prior to his decision to become a Fortune representative, Joel was a successful manager of a Fortune 100 company. He was miserable in this demanding role because he lacked financial independence and the freedom to manage his time as he chose.

As Joel came to understand the Fortune business model, he was impressed by the generous compensation plan and by the security the business provides. He jokes that working for Fortune is an opportunity no one can be downsized from. Joel's a fun-loving guy, but he's also dead-on serious in his desire to help others obtain what they want from Fortune as he strives toward reaching his ambitions.

Joel is determined to become a cash millionaire within the next few years and his aim is to retire before he turns forty. That thought has a familiar ring and I like his plan. I cheer for and offer support for all our representatives to reach that point of financial victory. I know how incredibly awesome that feeling will be for Joel and so many of our other representatives. I can tell you this much, "It's worth it, because the accomplishment absolutely makes life one hundred times better!"

There are certain things that we hold on to that represent little milestones in our lives. I've had so much help from so many throughout my journey. I have been blessed in every way. And by the way, I still have that 1995 Chevy Tahoe and it looks like it just came off the showroom floor. I have the oil changed about every five hundred miles and everyone around me knows how I feel about my Tahoe.

It seems every time I hop into my Tahoe I get that spine tingling, good feeling. The dreamer inside of me returns. I feel the excitement of being a kid again. It is such a rewarding feeling to know I am able to share my good fortune with so many people. I just smile. It's that feeling of winning, and it feels so good!

❋   ❋   ❋

13

CAN LIGHTNING STRIKE TWICE?

I RECEIVED A TELEPHONE CALL in the fall of 2000 as Tommy and I were in the formation stage of Fortune. Kenny Trout and Steve Smith, the founders of Excel, wanted to talk. They traveled to my home in Lexington. The meeting consisted of them encouraging me not to start Fortune. Basically, they said that my personal identity was Excel, and that it would be a very bad business decision on my part to step outside of that identity and try to do something else. "Paul, you've caught lightning in a bottle once. Lightning doesn't strike twice in the same place," Kenny warned.

I told them, "I don't think the new ownership of Excel sees the business opportunity the way I did, when I was doing well with the company. It just doesn't feel good for me to be a part of Excel at this time. I appreciate your concern, but I have to do what I feel is right for me."

The meeting ended with Kenny Trout walking out my front door saying, "Paul, what you are trying to do is business suicide. It won't work."

I have always believed God's favor is just around the corner in my life. If I just keep working harder, if I just don't give up, something good's gonna happen. I realize there is a master plan. My intent in getting back to work was to do what I hoped I could do, to help other people in some way. I believe what the Bible says, "To whom much is given, much is required." Everything that has happened in my life had to happen the way it did for me to be where I am today. The struggles and the hard knocks have led to my growth as a person and have given me a great appreciation for each step along the way.

> *My story is about an average guy who had a burning desire to succeed and do something big financially for himself and for his family, and who used network marketing to make it happen.*

I learned in growing up, while taking on a paper route and working on my father's paint crew, that work is good. Work is Scripture. It became clear to me in playing high school sports and college baseball that you have to fight and play hard on every play and you have to compete and play the entire game if you want to win.

When I had cancer, I was told by one physician that I had less than half a chance of living six months. Another physician told me if I did live, my life would never be normal. He was so right! Today, I'm not on any prescription drugs. Today, I'm not on any treatments. As a matter of fact, I haven't been back to the doctor or to a hospital for several years. My mind is clear. My purpose in life is strong. I feel better than I've ever felt.

I hope in reading this book people will be able to relate with a regular individual like me. I consider myself to have average intelligence with a life that has not been much different from anyone else's. We are all the same in many ways. We all have the same positive as well as negative thoughts. My story is about an average guy who had a burning desire to succeed and do something big financially for himself and for his family, and who used network marketing to make it happen.

Winning financially isn't easy. I realize that. Not everyone is willing to pay the price to win, and even some who are willing to pay the price for a while won't pay it long enough. I've said this so many times, "It's not who wants it the most, it's who wants it the longest." Winners in relationships, winners in their health life, winners in their spiritual life, actually winners in life, are the ones who are willing to pay the price until they win. Period.

✳   ✳   ✳

When I retired from Excel at the age of thirty-nine, I didn't feel like I was at the end of anything. I hadn't finished what I had really started. I had made some money, but that wasn't what all the hard times were about. I was really looking for something more. I once read, "If thou hast begun, go on. It is the end that crowns you, not the fight itself." I was itching to give back. I wanted to stay in the game; I wanted to build something better than before. It felt so right when Tommy and I decided to start this new business called Fortune.

Today, Fortune is a multi-million dollar company. We were highlighted in *Forbes* magazine as one of the top twenty-five emerging companies for the decade and were the only network marketing company listed. Many magazines have picked up on the explosive growth of our company. We have been featured in publications such as *Success From Home* and the *Millionaire Blueprint*. Several of our representatives have earned over a million dollars since joining the Fortune family. Many representatives are earning tens of thousands of dollars a month, and many more are earning the hundreds of extra dollars a month they were initially seeking.

I view Fortune as life with a pay plan. It includes all the bumps and bruises, highs and lows, the mountaintops and valleys of life, except it's associated with the Fortune pay plan. I always say, "Everybody out there is in the Fortune business." The real question is, "Are they in the Fortune pay plan?" Every day we all use the products that Fortune markets. Are we getting paid to use our cell phone? Are we getting paid when our friends and family use their cell phones, take nutritional supplements, watch television, or access the Internet? If not, we can!

I hope that Fortune is a company that offers the opportunity for someone to dream again. I think most people come into our type of business because it provides hope. You never know when you may come across somebody who knows a lot of people and understands the business and could be a real go-getter and do extremely well in this business. If you don't sign up you certainly won't find them, but if you do sign up you may. Wayne Gretzky once said, "You miss one hundred percent of the shots you don't take." I agree. If you're taking some shots in life, you certainly have a chance at doing something big.

Most people don't sign up to work hard in our business. I think it catches them by surprise. At first there's just a whole lot of hope that something good's gonna happen. Then you have a little success and something gets going. You have more success and you find that if you stick with it you end up working harder than you ever thought you would, because the financial rewards are bigger than you ever could have imagined.

We are bombarded in the media with how much tougher it is today to make it financially. All I know is it's easier today than it has ever been to make money in network marketing. We have voicemail, cell phones, text messaging, and the Internet. Fifteen years ago most people didn't have these luxuries. When I wanted to get in touch with people in Excel, I pulled off the road and called from a pay phone; they may have been home or they may not have been home.

I know the pitfalls out there in the field. I know what our representatives are up against every single day. I know there are those people who still say, "Network marketing, are you serious?" Many people believe and say, "If you've seen one network marketing company you've seen them all." I've lived through it. For those in our company, who are in the heat of

The bottom line is, we want the success of Fortune to be judged by how many millionaires we make.

the game, I know what they are up against. Therefore, I want them to have the best equipment possible to go out and compete for their families, and to win in their financial lives.

I am proud of the "equipment" we provide for our Fortune representatives. Our compensation plan is unparalleled in the industry. Today our representatives' sales growth ranks us as one of the fastest growing companies in the history of American business. We want every monetary record in network marketing to be broken by representatives of this company.

Tommy and I don't have any monetary goals for the Fortune company itself. We don't look at millions of dollars or billions of dollars of business for the future. We really don't. The key is to report each day and keep putting one foot in front of the other. Our aim is to make Fortune better and more efficient day after day. We don't measure the success of our business like a Wall Street company would, on a month-to-month basis or a quarterly basis. If Tommy and I had been leaders of a Wall Street-type company, after the first couple of years of our business we would have both been fired. Even today the company is not a bottom-line, profit-motivated business. Our company is profitable because of the fundamental structure we put in place from the get go. The bottom line is, we want the success of Fortune to be judged by how many millionaires we make.

Companies come and go and I'm fully aware of that. However, when Tommy and I talked and structured our business plan for Fortune, we specifically wanted to have no limits on what we could do in the future with our company. Fortune is tied to no one company, or industry or product. We are like a mutual fund-type marketing company because we have the safety of not being invested in just one stock. We have dozens of products with several different top-tier companies. So, if over a period of time the inevitable happens and a product goes out of favor or a business no longer offers a product or service our company markets, it will not have a major affect on any one specific Fortune business.

I would like to see all representatives in our company use Fortune to help them live a more balanced life. We can use the freedom of owning our own business to spend time with family. We can use the money we earn to help others. We don't need to spend everything we make in our business. We need to live beneath our means. If we make six, eight or ten thousand dollars a month and we spend every penny, we are no better off than the guy who is broke. If people can't live on ten thousand a month or twenty thousand a month, they won't be able to live on a hundred thousand a month.

I want our representatives to be financially independent with Fortune, and to plan for that time when they can be financially independent without Fortune. I also hope they plan for the time when they won't have the energy to rip and run and will financially prepare themselves for their retirement years. It's also important not to forget the giving part. While the money may leave your hands, it will never leave your life.

I am in the game I want to be in right now. I know life is short and we can take nothing for granted. I am able to focus on the part of my life that I want to focus on. I focus on progress instead of perfection. I focus on moving forward and on possibilities, instead of problems that could hold me back. In my business life my focus is on Fortune Hi-Tech Marketing. I believe Fortune offers the best opportunity for folks like us to make a big financial gain for ourselves and for our families.

I'm often asked, "How long will Fortune be around?" My response is, "Well, if the good Lord's willing, and if there is a need for commercials on the Super Bowl in the year 2020, then there will always be a need for Fortune." The companies paying out big bucks for those commercials are looking for customers, and that's what we do at Fortune. We gather customers for businesses. As long as companies are seeking customers for whatever products they market, there will be a need for Fortune. That means Fortune Representatives will be paid for the use of those products as long as those products are being used. That's money in Fortune Representatives' pockets today, tomorrow, in the year 2020 and beyond.

Fortune is not the only way to financial independence. Of course it's not; but it is a way. It is a way with almost no financial risk. Go-getters can do some really big stuff in their financial life with Fortune. The American dream is alive and well. Actually, I believe the American dream is more than alive and well. It's better than ever. The American dream, for those who work hard and position themselves in front of something big, is still very much alive.

It's simple really. I think multiplying people or multiplying money are the only two ways to make big money in this country. In our business, it so happens, we're multiplying people. So if someone doesn't have a lot of money, there's another way for people like me, Paul Orberson, a schoolteacher, to make a lot of money —and that is to multiply people. For those who are willing to pay the price, we want Fortune to be that company people turn to in order to win for themselves and for their family. That's what Fortune is all about—no more, no less.

✳   ✳   ✳

I never really modeled myself after anyone. Inevitably, though, people observe us. We observe others. I listen, I watch, I learn. I admire Michael Jordan's work ethic, and believe in his philosophy: "If you put in the work, the results will come. I don't do things half-heartedly because I know if I do, then I can expect half-hearted results." That is such a strong statement. Anything worth doing is worth doing right! We must combine who we are with what we learn from others in order to reach our full potential. Each of us knows what we don't want. Each of us still dreams big! Each of us is unique. I've heard it said and I believe it's true that when we are born the genius of heaven explodes.

I know I am the only person on this planet who controls my destiny. I know the story of my life is far from over. With hard work and the good Lord's help I have figured out that I decide when and where lightning will strike in my life.

I've researched lightning. It CAN strike twice in the same place!

✳   ✳   ✳

REFLECTIONS

by Tommy Mills

THREE BALLS AND TWO STRIKES in the bottom of the last inning with a runner on second base…I had faced the same situation the season before. Now, with two outs, I was in the batter's box again. I stood sixty feet, six inches away from the tough, left-handed pitcher from Boyle County, Paul Orberson. In my junior year, I came through with the game-winning hit for my Frankfort High Panther team and we won the Central Kentucky Conference Championship. Now a senior, I was determined for this game to end the same way. On the next pitch I hit the ball up the middle. My first thought was that I had another big hit for our team, but the second baseman, Paul's brother Mike, made a great backhanded catch and threw me out on a close play at first base. We lost the game, and Boyle County won the conference title that year.

Those battles between two very determined high school baseball players are my first memories of Paul Orberson. He threw hard and made the most of every pitch. He never gave in to a batter, working high, low, inside and out. Paul was certainly the best pitcher I batted against during my high school career.

At the time, I could not have imagined how our lives would intertwine, or envision the lifetime bond and friendship that would grow between us. Our first encounter came exactly the way it should have, through the competitive world of athletics. We would see each other again as opponents, when Paul pitched for Western Kentucky University and I played at Eastern Kentucky University.

Our paths led us both into teaching and coaching; I landed at Boyle County High School as the basketball coach. I wanted to move into administration and accepted a position as the Boyle County High School principal. My first responsibility was to hire a new basketball coach. The new coach needed to be someone who would treat the kids on my basketball team with respect and fairness, someone with a burning desire to succeed. I wanted someone who would work hard and focus his energy on developing young men, as well as good basketball players. I can remember thinking during Paul's interview, "If I had a son on next year's team, this is exactly the guy I would want to be his coach."

I literally chose a winner! While Paul was teaching and coaching I can remember him taking the team to get pizza after practice and buying shirts for the kids with his own money. He was always big-hearted and generous to people even before he was in a financial position to do so.

Paul and I developed a close friendship and soon realized that our backgrounds were very similar. My father was a teacher and athletic administrator, while Paul's dad was a teacher among the other jobs he held. We grew up in close-knit families centered around family activities. We both loved sports, and we quickly discovered that we shared a passion for business.

At that point in our lives, we were both looking for an opportunity to give our families more from a financial standpoint. We started by purchasing real estate together, which opened our eyes to another way of planning for our financial future. When Excel came along, we were receptive to the possibility of something different than the "9-5 routine" we had lived for so long. Paul and I developed a very close relationship during that period. We began to rely on each other's business instincts. We started believing in each other and appreciating how well we worked together. From the beginning, we have seemed to naturally share the responsibilities of any endeavor in which we are involved.

When Paul and I first joined Excel, we didn't really understand that much about it. We thought the big money was made on customer gathering. We rounded up our current and former basketball players to find people willing to switch their long distance phone services to Excel. After one weekend we had about twenty-five customers each, and we sent the paperwork into Excel. Unfortunately, Excel denied every single customer, because Danville did not yet allow its residents to choose their own long distance carrier. So, there was no opportunity to gather customers in our own hometown. Some people would have quit right there, but we didn't. We set up a big meeting in Frankfort at the Super 8 Motel. I invited people from my hometown and Paul thought he had a large group coming out to the meeting as well. We had cookies and punch, and I was all set to give the business presentation. We waited. We ate a lot of cookies and we waited. We drank a lot of punch and we waited, but no one showed. Most would have quit at this point, but we didn't.

Babe Ruth liked to say, "It's hard to beat a person that never gives up." When Paul sets his sights on something, he never gives up; he fights setbacks with more hard work. I know people look at his results and are quick to say that Paul was lucky. It was not luck! I was there.

I saw the hard work and every ounce of blood, sweat and tears. I saw the struggles he endured. I watched as he came to school each day, taught classes, went to basketball practice and then left in his old truck for an out-of-town meeting. I know there were many nights he didn't get home until two or three o'clock, only to return to school the next morning to do it all again. Paul made the Excel business work every step of the way. He willed it to work. He was determined not to give in, and he kept working until the only option was for his business to succeed. That is Paul Orberson. Everything Paul does, he does in a big way, to the very best of his ability. He goes full-throttle, full-speed ahead, on every project he undertakes.

I bought a piece of land close to town and built a home when I was still in the school business. I saw Paul in the middle of the week and mentioned that Saturday was moving day for me. There was a knock on my door at 7:00 a.m. on Saturday morning. Paul had his work clothes on and a truck in the driveway. Seeing him there at first was unexpected, but as I thought about it, I just smiled; that is exactly what I should have expected from Paul. We loaded and unloaded two small trucks over and over again and moved everything into my new house. It was close to midnight when we unloaded our last item and we were both worn out. I remember thinking, "Paul doesn't have to be here. He could have gone home hours ago and he would have still been helpful. I hadn't even asked him to help." But Paul is Paul—he wouldn't leave until the job was finished.

Paul has given time, energy, effort and more of whatever is needed for as long as I have known him. One December when I was the superintendent of the school system, Paul called and asked if I could choose two kids from each school in the county who may not have much for Christmas. I did. He picked up each of the kids in a stretch limousine and took them to Wal-Mart to shop for Christmas gifts for themselves, and for their entire families. I know the families of those children were really pleased and appreciative. I recall how "giddy" and happy that outing made Paul feel. He talked so much about those kids and the looks on their faces as they ran through Wal-Mart picking out gifts for their families. I believe that was one of those times Paul talks about, where the giver gets much more than the receiver.

Truly one of the worst days of my life was learning that Paul had cancer. My initial reaction was denial. He was in the office the week before with no indication that anything in the world could be wrong with him. The next thing I knew, the doctor told us he had a 50/50 chance of living for six months. Everything happened so fast. A couple of days after the diagnosis, he was in the hospital. A couple of days after that, he was in surgery. I went to see him every day in the hospital. I remember him being so weak and in a lot of pain. But even then, he maintained a positive attitude. He always asked about the business, how it was going, what needed to be done, or if there was anything he could do from his hospital bed. When he went back into the hospital the second time, I realized he was in a battle for his life.

I remember sitting in his dark hospital room listening to the doctors discuss ways to give Paul some hope. I was scared and worried. I wanted to be at the hospital as much as I could, but I knew how important it was to Paul for Fortune to stay strong and to keep moving forward. Jeff, the entire staff, and I worked to keep the office going, but things were not the same without Paul. I prayed every night that everything would work out.

I admired the courage Paul showed as he gave his heart and soul to his fight against cancer. Gradually, he made progress. Each step of the way, every time he met another recovery goal, he was proud and excited. We all were. His enthusiasm for life was contagious and rekindled the spirits of everyone around him.

In many ways, Paul has revealed his inner-self in this book. Those close to him, however, know there are so many things that he did not share. Paul is genuinely humble. For example, he would never tell the readers that while living in Florida, he received a fund-raising letter from his daughter's school for a new computer lab. He went to the school principal and laid down tens of thousands of dollars to completely pay for the entire project. He won't tell anyone how much he gives to his church on a regular basis. He won't share with the readers how he approached the University of Kentucky and "just wanted to help" with a million-dollar plus donation for new athletic offices. I guarantee that neither I, nor anyone else, really knows all of what Paul does for others every day of his life.

What Paul does share with the readers of this book are strategies and business building methods to help anyone get the most out of life. He challenges each one of us to get off our rumps and pursue our dreams. He shows us how hard knocks in life are normal, a part of the journey on the road to success. Paul said "yes" to a different way of life that evening in Brenda Hickey's basement. Through Fortune, Paul presents everyone with the opportunity to do something big financially for his or her family.

Today, Paul's ability to relate with our representatives in the field is what drives our Fortune business. He has such a great knack for being able to project the future needs of our representatives as they grow their businesses. He has a good feel for the effects any changes may have on their earning potential. As the leader of our company, he works and conducts his business exactly the way this book reads.

When WorldCom went bankrupt, Fortune was that company's number one customer gatherer. Jon Johnson, who had brought WorldCom to our company, was devastated on the morning after the bankruptcy announcement. In our meeting that day, Paul said, "Don't worry. Something good will come out of all this," and it did. We were the only company to receive the full amount WorldCom owed its creditors. It also proved the genius of Paul's business model. Tied to no one company, and no one industry, Fortune continued to move forward on the strength of our other product offerings.

When Paul asked me to write the forward for this book I was honored, but I said, "No." I didn't want to try and tell someone what I think about Paul and try to convince the reader that Paul is a great guy. I did agree to write these reflections. I wanted people to be able to form their own opinion by reading the book first. You have read Paul's words and have heard his story, as he tells it. I think the book is great. Paul shares his philosophy as he truly lives it on a daily basis. Work hard, keep your nose clean, do your best and don't ever give up: *Something Good's Gonna Happen.*

✳ ✳ ✳

PAUL'S VIEW

You don't have to be a special breed of dog to do something big with your life. You don't have to be born to the right kind of people, go to the right kind of school or grow up in the right neighborhood. *(Chapter 1, page 10)*

He always told us that God gives us what we need and God feeds the birds every morning, but He doesn't throw the worms down their throats. *(Chapter 1, page 10)*

In baseball, as well as in life, you have to play the entire game, from start to finish. *(Chapter 1, page 11)*

My father always told me that kids will remember how you treat them much longer than what you teach them. *(Chapter 1, page 14)*

Since then I've learned that in order to be truly successful, I must strive for balance in all areas of my life. *(Chapter 1, page 18)*

What is life? The Book of James is real clear: "Life is but a vapor that is here today and gone tomorrow." We all have that moment, a point when it hits us that life is temporary. *(Chapter 2, page 25)*

Network marketing provides equal opportunity. *(Chapter 3, page 32)*

Network marketing represents one of the last, great ways that a person with average ability, who has an above average desire to work, can accumulate great wealth. *(Chapter 3, page 32)*

There are two ways in this country to create wealth—to multiply money or to multiply people. If you don't have any money, then you better take a look at multiplying people. *(Chapter 3, page 33)*

This tells me that to make it big financially, personal desire and the commitment to do so are the most important factors. *(Chapter 3, page 35)*

It is only when we survive the tough times that we are able to realize the fruits of our labor. *(Chapter 3, page 37)*

Network marketing guarantees equal opportunities; it does not guarantee equal results. *(Chapter 3, page 39)*

The American dream is better than ever for people who work hard and position themselves properly in front of something big. *(Chapter 3, page 40)*

We can compete for financial independence, regardless of our education or our "place" in society. *(Chapter 3, page 40)*

Mark Twain once said, "The secret to getting ahead is to get started." *(Chapter 4, page 45)*

I don't think you need to know what you want out of life, because the things you want will change. I think you need to know exactly what you don't want out of life. *(Chapter 4, page 46)*

We all make up our minds to accept things as they are, or to change the things we don't want and start out on a new course. *(Chapter 4, page 47)*

In its simplest form, network marketing is actually a friendly conversation waiting to happen. I've found that my most cherished possessions over the years with network marketing experiences have been the relationships that I have formed and developed. *(Chapter 4, page 49)*

Hope is the feeling you get that the feeling you've got, ain't permanent. *(Chapter 4, page 50)*

…all the hoping and dreaming we do won't amount to a hill of beans if we don't take action. *(Chapter 4, page 50)*

I think sometimes we see other people who we think are successful and we say this or that about them, simply because we don't like where we are in our lives. *(Chapter 4, page 50)*

I've found that there is not that much difference in us doing something in a big way or in a small way. The bigger deal we make of it, the bigger deal it becomes. *(Chapter 4, page 51)*

Eleanor Roosevelt said, "Do the thing you fear and the death of fear is certain." *(Chapter 5, page 54)*

We are our own worst enemy. All of us can do something great if we just get out of our own way. We underestimate our greatest opponent in life: ourselves. *(Chapter 5, page 55)*

By not making a decision to do something else, I made a decision to keep on doing what I was doing. *(Chapter 5, page 55)*

It's not that we can't do great things; it's just that we won't attempt to do great things. *(Chapter 5, page 56)*

Our enemy could be life issues such as maintaining good health, balancing finances, developing good relationships or settling family issues. We only conquer the giants in our lives by facing our fears head on. *(Chapter 5, page 57)*

Get over it, because nothing will keep you more emotionally, physically and financially broke than constantly thinking about the past. *(Chapter 5, page 57)*

"Yesterday's history, tomorrow's a mystery, today is all we've got and it's a gift from God. That is why today is called the present." *(Chapter 5, page 60)*

What price are we willing to pay to secure something that is really important to us? *(Chapter 6, page 63)*

There can't be a testimony in life without a test! *(Chapter 6, page 65)*

So often we fail to credit ourselves for the tests in our lives that we have successfully passed. My goodness, every single one of us has come through difficult struggles and come out better for it on the other side. *(Chapter 6, page 66)*

Whether things are perceived to be real or whether they are real, it's just the same. If you think it, then you better believe it's real. *(Chapter 6, page 67)*

Fear, I've learned, is nothing more than premeditated failure. *(Chapter 6, page 68)*

What is the secret to happiness? I don't know, but I do know the secret to misery is trying to make sure everyone around you is happy. *(Chapter 6, page 69)*

We need to look at the bigger picture of our whole life and not just that knothole view of a single problem at the moment. *(Chapter 6, page 70)*

I've found that most of us know what we need to do in life, but most often it's the thing that we least want to do, that is the very next thing we need to do. *(Chapter 7, page 75)*

…over the years I developed a three-step checklist that helped me: (1) I looked for "people, people." … (2) I sought people with credibility in their community; and (3) I looked for people who were in need of some additional income. *(Chapter 7, page 77)*

I learned by not begging and harassing, I saved my enthusiasm for the business and lived to fight another day. *(Chapter 7, page 77)*

When we introduce our business, we are not only talking to that person, but we are also talking to everybody that person knows. *(Chapter 7, page 78)*

Never underestimate the potential of what you view as bad days to turn into really good days. *(Chapter 7, page 80)*

Every time I presented the program or talked to someone about Excel, I thought about Roscoe and Jim. The person I was talking to may not be interested, but someone they knew just might! *(Chapter 7, page 81)*

In network marketing our goal is to elevate, uplift and help as many people as possible. The only way for our business to grow is to help someone else in this business to succeed. *(Chapter 7, page 81)*

The network marketing business is not rocket science. …It's doing the simple things and applying the discipline to get things done that builds a successful business. *(Chapter 7, page 82)*

Good things come to those who go after what the other fellow sits back and waits for. As we assemble our business, we must do today what others will not do, so that we may have tomorrow what others will not have. *(Chapter 7, page 82)*

"When you get so tired that you think about giving up or quitting what you are doing, think about looking your youngest child in the eye and saying, 'I don't have the courage to win for you.'" *(Chapter 8, page 97)*

… we all must be accountable to someone. We must be accountable to our families, or our church, or our charitable mission. We must stand up and be willing to give an account of ourselves whatever our purpose may be. *(Chapter 8, page 98)*

Life on this earth ain't forever. …Live life with purpose! There is more to us being here than just breathing and taking up space. If you're not living life on the edge, then you're taking up too much space. *(Chapter 8, page 99)*

This business is not about how much we want it. It's really not. It's about how long we want it. We don't need any special talent or skills to succeed in network marketing, just the desire. *(Chapter 8, page 99)*

Success is all about "want to." *(Chapter 8, page 99)*

We all have those thoughts of doubt. Doubt is perfectly normal, yet I've found that winners act in spite of doubt. We are not always going to be full of faith, but winners act in spite of their lack of faith. *(Chapter 8, page 102)*

The best thing to do when we overeat is not to give up on a healthy diet or give up on the whole program, but to return to the healthy lifestyle the next day. *(Chapter 8, page 102)*

Doubts can be overcome when we hold on to that constant feeling that no matter the current circumstance, something good's gonna happen in our life. *(Chapter 8, page 102)*

Residual income is the income generated from the continued use of the products used by customers month after month. *(Chapter 8, page 103)*

Furthermore, in our traditional work roles, we only receive pay for the work we produce individually. The networking industry allows us to build a team of colleagues and for us to share monetarily in the success of hundreds and even thousands of people. *(Chapter 8, page 104)*

We should all strive to carry minimal debt or no debt at all. *(Chapter 9, page 107)*

Fundamentals are called fundamentals in every aspect of life, and while stressing the basics in basketball or football may not be the greatest of fun, the fun part comes with the results: winning! *(Chapter 9, page 109)*

Somebody who leaves our lives never controls our destiny. Don't fight it—there is always a plan. *(Chapter 9, page 113)*

We all know there are certain things we need to separate ourselves from in order to maximize our capabilities. Before we can be promoted in life, we must separate ourselves from what has gone on before. *(Chapter 9, page 113)*

We don't control our habits; our habits control us. The key is to make sure our habits are good ones. *(Chapter 9, page 114)*

Fundamentally, networking is about going out and meeting people. It's about doing the things we say we are going to do—if we say we are going to meet someone at Shoney's, be on time and meet them there—fundamentally treat people as you would have them treat you. *(Chapter 9, page 115)*

Achieving success in this business is not so much about being a great speaker or possessing higher intellect. I think it's more about being able to relate to people. *(Chapter 9, page 115)*

It really is easier to give birth in our business than it is to raise the dead. *(Chapter 9, page 116)*

...as a person striving to build our business, we only have a limited amount of time. We must spend that precious time with people who are willing to pay somewhat of a price to win. *(Chapter 9, page 116)*

If we are in business to make money, then the fundamentals of our business tell us we have to spend our time where we think it is going to reward our business the most. *(Chapter 9, page 117)*

To be successful in business, our focus must always be on the other person. *(Chapter 10, page 120)*

People have to know how much you care, before they care how much you know. *(Chapter 10, page 121)*

There are times we need to let those around us hear that we don't know everything, and times they need to hear that they don't either. *(Chapter 10, page 121)*

We can't make all people fit all roles for all occasions; it's just not possible. *(Chapter 10, page 122)*

As leaders we can help identify the areas where individuals in our organization are strong and work together to build a much more effective team. *(Chapter 10, page 122)*

We become successful leaders when we combine our past experiences and accomplishments with the dreams and the passion we hold for the future. *(Chapter 10, page 124)*

We want to learn from successful people in all walks of life, and especially from those who are doing well in our business. But we can't change who we are or try to become something we're not in our effort to chase success. *(Chapter 10, page 124)*

I have no doubt in my mind that the givers of this world sleep better at night, have a more positive outlook on the day ahead, are more healthy, and live a fuller life than those who are not givers. *(Chapter 11, page 133)*

Yes, I would be nothing without His grace and love for me. Beyond all of that thankfulness, though, we've still got to get off our rear ends and do our share of the workload! *(Chapter 11, page 134)*

Giving is the living proof that the cancer of greed hasn't eaten our souls. *(Chapter 11, page 139)*

If I can encourage anything at all in this book it would be for us all to give as we go. *(Chapter 11, page 139)*

When we are kids we place no limits on the possibilities that are ahead of us…As kids we dream big! We dream of living in castles, of being kings and queens, of reaching higher, going further and of accomplishing whatever our imaginations tell us we can accomplish. *(Chapter 12, page 144)*

We say to our kids, "Follow your dreams!…" …yet we aren't out there pushing to become everything we want to be. We aren't out there chasing our dreams. *(Chapter 12, page 145)*

Pursuing our dreams is what makes life, life! *(Chapter 12, page 146)*

Martin Luther King, Jr. stated it best: "Everyone can be great because anybody can serve. You don't have to have a college degree to serve. You don't have to make your subject and your verb agree to serve. You only need a heart full of grace, a soul generated by love." *(Chapter 12, page 147)*

I have always believed God's favor is just around the corner in my life. If I just keep working harder, if I just don't give up, something good's gonna happen. I realize there is a master plan. *(Chapter 13, page 153)*

I believe what the Bible says, "To whom much is given, much is required." *(Chapter 13, page 154)*

Winning financially isn't easy. I realize that. Not everyone is willing to pay the price to win, and even some who are willing to pay the price for a while won't pay it long enough. *(Chapter 13, page 155)*

Winners in relationships, winners in their health life, winners in their spiritual life, actually winners in life, are the ones who are willing to pay the price until they win. **Period.** *(Chapter 13, page 155)*

Wayne Gretzky once said, "You miss one hundred percent of the shots you don't take." *(Chapter 13, page 156)*

If we make six, eight or ten thousand dollars a month and we spend every penny, we are no better off than the guy who is broke. *(Chapter 13, page 158)*

It's also important not to forget the giving part. While the money may leave your hands, it will never leave your life. *(Chapter 13, page 158)*

The American dream, for those who work hard and position themselves in front of something big, is still very much alive. *(Chapter 13, page 159)*

✳　　✳　　✳

ACKNOWLEDGMENTS

When I decided to pay the price to win financially, those closest to me paid a price too. My family and friends get very little credit for the good things that have happened in my life. They don't receive any of the glory, and yet they have sacrificed as much or perhaps more than I ever have.

For many years, my children, Sarah and Jeffrey, endured more than anyone. I am so thankful for their unconditional love and I hope they realize that I love them more than I could ever put into words. I am so very proud to be their "daddy".

I am grateful to my former wife, Carla, the mother of Jeffrey and Sarah. She conducted our household under very stressful conditions and raised two really great kids. She is a terrific mom.

I especially thank my wife, Sheryl, who has been so wonderful as our dedication to the Fortune business continues. I appreciate so much the patience, support and love that I receive from Brian, Shannon and her.

My "story" would not be much to read about if not for the help of so many people along the way. I have been blessed beyond my imagination with good relationships and lasting friendships, for which I am eternally grateful.

I want to thank my father for showing me the benefits of a strong work ethic. To my mother and father, thank you for raising me in a God-honoring home.

I am thankful for Dr. Bob Baker. His friendship, wisdom and love for the Lord inspire me daily to be a better person. I am so appreciative of Don Lane for his honesty, integrity and the encouragement he provides. His sincere friendship means so much in my life.

Thanks to my sister, Karen, who has been good to me as well as good for me. She has truly hung in there with me over the years. Her husband, Barry Levy, is dedicated to the success of Fortune and has always been supportive of everything I have done. I appreciate them both.

I would also like to offer a great big thanks to David and Randy Mills. Without their help this book could not have been written. I've really enjoyed our collaborative sessions. I appreciate their effort, their patience, and the vast number of hours they have given to this book project. Also, a special thanks to Sue Thomas Warren for her support and her work during the editing phase of *Something Good's Gonna Happen*.

I thank Tommy Mills for being here. I'm not sure if it makes any sense to anyone else, but my best friend simply makes every day of my life run smoother. We have faced some pretty serious bumps in the road, but I've always counted on Tommy to even out the ride.

Everything good in life happens with the help of others. So it has been in my life and so it is with this book. I realize the game of life is much like any board game we play: at some point, all the pieces must go back into the box. I brought nothing into this world; I will take nothing with me. I will be judged on what I have done for others.

Paul Orberson